YOUR
Exhilarating
LIFE

CREATING PROSPERITY
IN FAMILY AND CAREER

CARMEL D. BROWN

ARNICA PRESS

The material contained in this book has been written for
informational purposes and is not intended as a substitute
for medical advice, nor is it intended to diagnose, treat, cure,
or prevent disease. If you have a medical issue or illness,
consult a qualified physician.

Published by ARNICA PRESS
www.ArnicaPress.com

© 2020 Carmel D. Brown
www.carmelbrowncounseling.com

Cover photo by Kostenko Maxim

ISBN: 978-1-7352446-5-5

YOUR
Exhilarating
LIFE

CREATING PROSPERITY
IN FAMILY AND CAREER

CARMEL D. BROWN

For Rodney

TABLE OF CONTENTS

ACKNOWLEDGMENTS

I am truly grateful to my husband Rodney with whom I have been able to create such a great life. Thanks for allowing me to write, create, learn, and build while providing support, encouragement, and love. You have always believed in me, our predestined journey together and the power of true love. You have continued to support my dreams and goals and have always found a way to make them happen for me. Thanks for being my dominion partner, best friend, and the love of my life. Let's continue creating memories and building this wonderful life together.

INTRODUCTION

In your hands you are holding a very unique book! The information provided is intended for current business owners or aspiring business owners that desire to succeed. I am pleased to share my personal and professional experience, and expertise to help you achieve success in the most important areas of life. When read thoroughly and applied properly, the material included will help you discover, develop and launch your true calling and live a life of prosperity.

This book provides an unusual compilation of information, tools, and strategies to assist the reader with achieving emotional balance, mental and physical wellness, inspiration, clear guidance, and includes business savvy advice. Most importantly, you will learn how to identify personal deficits and flaws, and correct them so that they don't get in the way of your opportunities to succeed in life. Business ownership and entrepreneurship are largely based on hard work, commitment, and relationships. Therefore, failing to achieve emotional stability, wellness, balance, and a healthy relationship with yourself could hinder the ability to commit, complete the work required, and maintain healthy business and professional relationships. Succeeding at life entails more than making money or becoming well-known. Success is more enjoyable when you love yourself, have healthy relationships, achieve a sense of purpose, and are mentally and physically healthy. Get ready to learn and apply all that I offer so that you too can start your journey to a life of happiness, wellness, and prosperity.

There are many individuals in our society who are physically healthy and have put in hours, months, and years to sculpt a picture-perfect physique. Bodybuilding professionals and competitors are very present on social media, in magazines, and other digital and print media platforms. Unfortunately, some of these very same individuals neglect their mental health and use exercise as their only coping skill. Exercise is certainly therapeutic, a healthy coping skill, and a great tool for managing and improving both mental and physical health. However, acquiring additional tools and developing other areas is essential and critical for a fulfilling and successful life. If your physical health and appearance become the only leg you have to stand on, you will eventually find that this is a recipe for failure, because our physical appearance and condition slowly change over time. Some of these changes can be good, depending on how well you take care of yourself and what your habits are as you age.

Many people are healthier and in better shape in their later years than they were in their younger years. Unfortunately for many, it is because they were diagnosed with some sort of a health condition and were forced to follow a healthier lifestyle in order to prevent premature death. Another reason to have more than exercise as a coping skill is that there might come a time in your life when you can't exercise due to illness, injury, or a life altering circumstance. The goal is always to prevent such situations from occurring, however we don't always get to choose our life circumstances. If you don't have access to that one coping mechanism during a challenging time, you might experience an increased risk for deterioration in your mental health or symptoms of depression.

Studies show that there is a correlation between mental illness and poor physical health. If one is struggling with symptoms of mental illness or any type of emotional instability, they could eventually experience deterioration of their physical health. Sadness, low self-esteem, failed relationships, and low job satisfaction may impede or reduce energy level and motivation to exercise which will accelerate deterioration of physical health. Similarly, an individual with mental health concerns that does not take care of their physical health, could eventually begin to experience deterioration in their mental health condition. For example, failure to exercise, eat healthy, and adopt a healthy lifestyle could result in obesity, and other physical health problems. Ultimately, an individual who becomes physically ill or unhealthy increases their risk for experiencing symptoms of depression, anxiety, isolation, and decreased quality of life. In addition, living with obesity or other physical health problems can result in lack of confidence and low self-esteem. Living your best life involves more than exercise, a healthy diet, and stable mental health.

> *It is impossible to be the best version of yourself,*
> *and truly happy, unless you are physically, mentally,*
> *and spiritually healthy, have healthy relationships,*
> *as well as meaningful work.*

Mental and physical health affects other major areas of your life. The risk for deterioration in mental and physical health are significantly increased when an individual has not acquired the ability to maintain healthy interpersonal relationships, not engaged in meaningful work, and their life is not consistent with their purpose.

Eventually, individuals may develop depression and anxiety, which may in turn result in lack of motivation for exercise and poor eating habits. Fitness, nutrition, career satisfaction, mental health, and interpersonal relationships impact each other in a very critical manner. When one area is negatively impacted, the other areas are at risk of deterioration.

This is what inspired Rodney and I to create *Your Exhilarating Life*. As young, busy professionals and parents we were both significantly overweight prior to beginning our health and fitness journey. We had great careers, a healthy marriage, and were both in good mental health, but struggled with fitness and nutrition. This impacted other areas of our life. Being overweight makes you tired, so we weren't as active as we would like to have been. I had always eaten slightly healthier than the average young person in early adulthood and exercised regularly, but not enough to prevent being overweight. Genetically I was predisposed to being overweight.

> ## YOUR EXHILARATING LIFE
> *is a life transformation program that focuses on*
> *each participant's goals in the following core areas:*
>
> *Family and interpersonal Relationships*
> *Mental Health and Emotional Well-being*
> *Confidence and Self-esteem*
> *Business and Career*
> *Fitness and Nutrition*

In this book we will learn about each of these crucially important components.

When I work with my clients that are enrolled in our program, they each receive personal coaching, business mentorship, ongoing counseling, fitness training, nutrition and healthy lifestyle guidance, and a sense of connectedness that allows them to thoroughly develop and improve each of these five core areas. This program has proven that satisfaction in core areas of one's life results in overall increased contentment with life. A positive chain reaction assures a sense of purpose, increased happiness, improved mental and physical health, enhanced productivity, and fulfilling interpersonal relationships. When these core areas are strengthened, the individual is empowered and confident to live a fulfilling, successful and happy life.

Increasing the number of individuals who are successful, healthy, and happy in our society will ultimately reduce crime, divorce and unemployment, while strengthening communities, and significantly improving the health, stability, and strength of our nation as a whole.

Isn't it true that a large percentage of individuals that live a life of intentional and habitual crime have unstable employment, unhealthy interpersonal relationships, and typically aren't the happiest or healthiest people? Do most communities that are thriving, full of life, have low crime rates, and continuously growing, consist of generally happy and healthy people? Are these the communities where the individuals spend more time outside, engaging in physical activity such as exercise, yard work, and property maintenance? Do they consist of two parent families, rather than a large percentage of single parent families? Do most residents have education and careers? If the answer to these questions is YES, then it is highly likely that my statement is true. Creating a program such as *Your Exhilarating Life,* which aims to increase the number of individuals who are successful, healthy, and happy, will promote lower crime rates. It will also significantly reduce divorce and unemployment rates. As a result, it will promote stability, as well as improve the overall health of our communities and our nation as a whole.

Achieving your best life is difficult, there will be failures, and it will take endurance. I will cover many of our most significant challenges in each of the core areas. In this book I share our journey to our best life yet! Read along and get empowered to live!

PART I:

FAMILY AND INTERPERSONAL RELATIONSHIPS

I.

Chapter I.
Mental Health and Emotional Well - Being

Deal with Yourself First

It is imperative that you work through your unresolved issues before you open a business, start a family, or help others. This is also necessary in order to reduce the amount of damage and potential harm to your professional and personal relationships. Many people get in their own way and prevent themselves from progressing and achieving their professional goals, due to arrogance and failure to admit when they are wrong, easily offended, and lack emotional intelligence. If you don't deal with your personal issues and shortcomings, you will find yourself stagnant and spinning your wheels.

> *In order to succeed in life, it isn't mountains*
> *but mainly ourselves that we must conquer.*

Some of the most important aspects of conquering yourself are identifying your flaws and weaknesses, sharpening your skills, strengthening areas in which you have deficits, and addressing any present problems with mental health, self-esteem, or insecurities. Failure to engage in ongoing self-evaluation will make it impossible to reach your full potential, you will get in your own way, and lose very important friendships and partnerships. Many people in leadership positions lie to themselves and others about the true state of their emotional health, due to fear of being judged, disrespected, or embarrassed. If you are walking into the best years of your life but are having episodes of untreated deep and dark depression, you might be setting yourself up for failure. Health challenges such as Anxiety, Depression, Bipolar and other mood disorders are fairly common and easily treated with therapy and medication, if necessary. In addition, you will not function optimally if you fail to address your mental health status, are unable to regulate emotions during times of distress and manage your symptoms. You could potentially ruin significant opportunities and important relationships. Sometimes there is no basis for clinical diagnosis, but an inability to manage anger and other emotions, effectively communicate and resolve conflict, can be harmful to your career and relationships.

There are many facets to dealing with yourself first and dealing with unresolved personal issues. One area that is not mentioned enough is refraining from getting involved on the rebound. We hear of this being an important principle in intimate relationships, but unfortunately no one warns us of how this relates to business relationships. If you have been in abusive or unhealthy relationships, friendships, or partnerships, it will put you at risk for carrying that baggage to the next relationship. For example, if your significant other in your last relationship had an affair and you get into another relationship on the rebound without first allowing yourself to heal from those old wounds, it could be very difficult for you to trust your new partner or have a healthy relationship with them. You will bring a great deal of toxicity into your new relationship. The same is true for business partnerships. Leaving a business partnership after a big disagreement or an unhealthy partnership, where you were outright mistreated, sets you up for failure in the next collaboration if you don't deal with unresolved issues from the previous partnership.

Entering into a business partnership with someone else after you have experienced a failed partnership or relationship, or on the rebound, puts you at risk of having to pay for the damage done in the previous partnership. Allow yourself time to reflect on the events that occurred, why they happened what role you played in those events, and what you can do to prevent the same incidents from occurring in future partnerships. After being regularly abused or mistreated in a relationship of any kind for a long period of time, your self-esteem becomes low. You may become bitter, have a hard time trusting others, or feel the need to "one-up" your new partner while competing with them. As a consequence, you may have the unfortunate desire to hurt others before they get a chance to hurt you in future relationships or partnerships. This is a recipe for disaster.

Give yourself time for self-evaluation, reflection, and most importantly time to heal before sealing the deal with a new business or intimate partner.

Statistics suggest one in four Americans ages 18 and older suffer from a diagnosable mental health disorder. If the disorder is diagnosable it is treatable. Most individuals can proceed through life in a healthy and successful manner with a mental illness as long as they follow treatment recommendations, communicate with treatment providers, and take care of themselves. Treatment recommendations vary depending on the providers therapeutic approach, diagnosis, client goals for treatment, and history.

It is important to become familiar with family history to determine if you are at risk for developing a mental illness. Knowing your risk factors ahead of time helps with prevention and early intervention. Ignoring risk factors and early warning signs can result in loss of control, due to unmanaged symptoms. Loss of control could consist of an episode in which hurtful words are spoken, resulting in termination of employment, performance issues, ruining professional reputation or your personal relationships. A great place to start is medication compliance, if recommended by prescriber and remaining consistent with therapy sessions and self-care. We have a history of stigma where mental illness is concerned however, this has improved over the years. Several celebrities, professionals, and successful leaders have publicly revealed their personal struggles with mental illness. This has been helpful in removing stigma and encouraged others to seek professional help. Seeking professional help and remaining compliant with treatment recommendations increases the likelihood of long-term success in personal happiness, business, and relationships.

Finally, it is crucial that we understand the importance of taking care of our mental, as well as physical health. Typically when a person is in pain, they want nothing more than to get rid of the pain. Having the same approach with mental and emotional pain could save a lot of lives, result in healthier interpersonal and business relationships, and improve your quality of life. That excruciating sadness, inability to relax or focus, and mood instability are just as critical as physical pain and we should treat it as such. Make an appointment with your primary care provider or a psychiatrist for prescribed medication. Visit a licensed mental health provider for therapy and further treatment. These two decisions will provide you with the opportunity to feel better, perform better at work, have healthier relationships, and the advantage to remain on task with goals.

II.

CHAPTER II.
CONFIDENCE AND SELF - ESTEEM

Believe in yourself because if you don't, no one else will.
Whether you think you can
or whether you think you can't, you're right.
~ Henry Ford ~

A healthy self-image, confidence, and self-esteem are not qualities we can learn in a classroom. They are achieved by surpassing self-set limitations, learning to like ourselves, expecting respect from others, setting standards and boundaries for how we desire to be treated, cultivating self-acceptance, and being okay with the fact that not everyone will like us. Learning to love and accept yourself is a prerequisite to having healthy relationships with others, being emotionally healthy, and enjoying a successful life. Self-love is not only necessary for personal happiness, it is also a prerequisite for loving others.

Self-love, self-worth, and self-respect
start with the word SELF
simply because you can't acquire them from anyone else,
as they come from within.

Whether or not we love ourselves not only determines how we see ourselves, it also determines how we think others see us. It also affects our overall worldview. Regardless of what mistakes you have made, how others have treated you, and whether others value you, it is important that you choose to love yourself, believe you are valuable, and expect respect from others. This is critical for your emotional well-being

We live in a society that stands to gain great profits from our self-doubt and poor sense of self. Bookstores and online retailers have loads of reading material focused on helping us achieve happiness. The decision to like yourself is somewhat of a rebellious act in such a time as this. I strongly encourage rebellion in this matter. Think of how much money we would save as a society, if people loved and accepted themselves regardless of circumstances. Many of us invest in expensive material items because we believe they say, "I am someone important." This is one of the reasons many people buy expensive cars they can't afford, wear expensive clothes and handbags they can't afford, take trips they can't afford, buy houses they can't afford, and live above their means. Quite often, people believe the label or the price of these items makes them important or adds value to who they are. Make no mistake, many people buy expensive items because they have worked hard to secure income and resources that allows them to have such a lifestyle. This applies to someone who is wearing $200 shoes, carrying $500 handbags, but does not own anything, while barely keeping on their utilities, and drowning in debt.

How do you know if you love yourself? What you tell yourself about you, or your self-talk is one of the most important indicators as to whether you love yourself or not. For example, if you are telling yourself things such as: " I am such a loser, I can't get anything right, I can't get ahead, I'm ugly, I'm fat, no one wants me, no one loves me, this is the best I'll ever do, I am too old, I am not smart enough, or my life is pointless," you are engaging in negative and self-defeating self-talk. This is not indicative of self-love. In addition, if you allow other people to disrespect you, abuse you, or take advantage of you while you continue seeking their approval or pursue their friendship, you clearly don't love yourself. In other words, chasing people whose behavior towards you is disrespectful or hurtful, results in more emotional pain and feelings of failure. The abusive person has more opportunities to reject you as long as you continue allowing them into your space and are seeking their approval. Each time they criticize you, abuse you, or reject you, it has a negative impact on your emotional well-being. This results in negative self-talk and impedes progress toward self-acceptance.

> *Love yourself, respect yourself, and believe in yourself*
> *so others will love you, believe in you, and respect you.*
> *The way you treat yourself sets a standard*
> *for how others will treat you.*

Once you begin loving yourself, you will see an immediate improvement in confidence and self-esteem. Confidence is critical for achieving success in any area of life. In most cases it isn't who you are that holds you back from being successful, it's who you think you are not. Many people will try to make you think that having a high self-esteem and being self-confident is prideful. It is not the same thing as pride or arrogance. In fact, it is the exact opposite. When a person is self-confident, they are capable of listening to others, empathizing and accepting them as equals, as well as forgiving and celebrating them. Learning to refrain from saying anything about yourself that you don't want to come true, will help you maintain confidence, hence accomplish your goals and dreams. Negative thinking, self-doubt, and insecurity are dream killers, so pay attention to the way you talk to yourself. Verbalize who you are, believe who you are, and BE who you are.

One day I sat and thought about a few well-known leaders as well as a few local leaders that I follow or know personally. I evaluated their life's work and how they became known as leaders. I realized that most of them accomplished that simply by being themselves and sharing their gift and knowledge with others. They were confident that what they had to offer was valuable, they told themselves they were leaders, they believed they were leaders, and they told us they were leaders. As a result, we believed it as well. I am not referring to any average Joe that has not put in the necessary work to be deserving of the role as leader. The leaders that I am referring to have impressive resume's and certainly did the work to earn the title. My point is that there are so many others that have earned it as well but lack in confidence, therefore fail to walk into the leadership role. Your thoughts and words about yourself profoundly impact who you become. Most great leaders simply believed their work made them great, shared this with us, and we bought in.

I realized that most of them wouldn't be considered leaders by the public, had they not told themselves they were leaders and believed it first. This resulted in a change in mindset for me. I didn't need to wait on someone to label me a leader, because what I did every day suggested I already was one. I was an educated business owner, a successfully published author, I had been asked to appear for speaking engagements on various occasions, was coaching numerous people, and personally mentored several individuals on private and business goals. Various professionals have asked for my assistance in helping them open their business or practice, while providing them with important information and resources. I advised hundreds on how to maintain a healthy marriage, overcome the challenges of parenting, and many other important facets of their lives.

Although I'd provided such leadership time and time again, I had never referred to myself as a leader. I simply didn't market myself as an expert in business, relationships, or life transformations. Behind the scenes I was quietly consulting with aspiring business owners regarding starting their clinical practices and businesses as they approached me with questions and direction. I was helping people transform their lives on demand, without hesitation and regularly because that is who I am, who I was created to be, and what I am good at. I am a leader. It took me many years to say this out loud. Like many other experts, I thought someone else had to give me that title. I have observed organizations, religious groups, and other entities appoint their leaders and executive staff, and give them big titles. I finally realized I was the only one that could give myself a title to describe who I was created to be. I am a natural born leader rather than a self-appointed leader, as leadership was never my goal or intention. This is the truth that I can no longer hide from, therefore I have decided to speak it, claim it, live it, believe it, and share it.

> *Accepting your assignment and title given by God*
> *is not just about who you are.*
> *It's just as much about who you think*
> *and believe you are, and who you say you are.*

It is time you step into your role as well and confess your title. Who were you created to be? Who are you? Have you discovered your assignment and claimed it?

27

Decide today that you are valuable, for there is no amount of money or materialism that can take that away or add to it. You have to decide you are valuable with or without your possessions. If all of the "stuff" was stripped away from you today, would you lose all confidence in yourself and your ability? Would you no longer be a leader, successful or valuable if you lost your house? Filed bankruptcy? Had no money in the bank? Didn't have a car? Time and time again we have seen people lose it all, which makes it a reality that could happen to anyone.

> *The Lord giveth and the Lord taketh away.*
> *~ Job 1:21 ~*

If your value is wrapped up in your material possessions and somehow those things are suddenly gone, where does that leave you? Worthless? Invaluable? Vow today that you are inherently valuable, and the material possessions, education, relationships, connections, and achievements are just added bonuses. Be confident and speak success and value over your life and self-image.

Having acknowledged my personal imperfections, I can better identify and address unresolved issues. I am emotionally intelligent enough to refrain from allowing unresolved conflict to interfere with my ability to support my clients. I can serve customers, lead my staff and supervisees, effectively mentor my mentees, and be the best business and life partner possible. I want the same for you!

III.

CHAPTER III.
COMPETING AND COMPARING

Comparing yourself to others is one definite way to create and perpetuate low self-esteem and failure. Failure is a part of life, however, some failure is unnecessary and avoidable. As long as you compare yourself to others, you will never measure up. When your self-esteem is low, or you believe that you are not enough, you won't perform well, and therefore not effectively serve your life's purpose. After our fitness center was open and running for a year, I remember someone telling me what another fitness studio owner was doing in our area. The person asked if I had ever been to the other studio's website or social media page. My response was, "No, I haven't been to their website or page, because I don't want to get so caught up in what they are doing, that I start competing and lose sight of our mission and purpose." I then told them that the fitness professionals that I follow online are not in our immediate area. Therefore I wouldn't find myself competing with them, losing confidence because they are doing something I am not, or they have more clients than I do. Of course, I had to evaluate the market in my area and analyze the competition prior to opening.

Once our business was open, I stopped paying attention to what some might consider my competition was doing. Instead, I started focusing on my goals, purpose, and intentions.

29

I was in a race all by myself, as if I had a wall up on each side of me, preventing me from seeing the progress my competitors in the lanes next to me were making. I couldn't tell and didn't care if they were ahead of me or behind me, because their race is theirs to win and my race is personal as well. I wasn't competing with them because I am my only competition.

Unfortunately, it is very easy to get pulled into the competition of life, or what many of us refer to as the "rat race." I have seen many people do it. It is exhausting and not something I ever want to be a part of.

> *No matter how great you are,*
> *there will always be someone greater, better,*
> *more attractive, more qualified, smarter,*
> *or more successful.*
> *So why waste your time worrying about that?*

When you observe others are competing with you or comparing themselves to you, be sure not to get pulled into that dynamic. This is simply a distraction and will get you off track.

Competing and comparing can impede success as you might find yourself more focused on the people you are competing and comparing yourself with, than actually working on your goals and being productive. There will be many people publishing their books, opening businesses, obtaining college degrees, after seeing you as an example. Some will follow your path simply because you inspired them to do so, and this should be exactly what we want to see.

If you are a leader, you should want to have such an impact on others, that they are empowered to write books, apply for promotions, open businesses, get married, save their marriages, be better parents and spouses, or achieve some of the things that you have achieved. We can't market ourselves as helpers, coaches, leaders and mentors, but get mad when someone else produces something great. After seeing your work, some might initiate endeavors, because they believe they can do it better than you. They will be competing. Some will write and publish books, begin a weight loss or body transformation journey, start businesses, obtain a college education, get married, and a slew of other things, because they believe they can do it better than you. It is very unfortunate that people do these things for unhealthy reasons rather than the right reason, but that is absolutely none of your business.

When other people attempt to copy your lifestyle or business model, take it as a compliment rather than getting angry. I call this "franchising." Many people will never progress beyond "mom and pop" status because they spend too much energy trying to keep their style and business practices a secret, due to fear of being outdone or outworked, while large entities are trying to sell their model for profit and notoriety.

> *What's the point in finding the secret*
> *or solution to anything that matters*
> *and keeping it to yourself?*

If that were the case, we wouldn't have textbooks or school. After all, isn't that all school is? People teaching new generations information that someone else discovered or created? The creators and founders of the information that flows through the textbooks we study, sold that information or "franchised" it for a profit. Had they kept it to themselves, their work would not be shared across the world, and they wouldn't have experienced the success that comes with sharing that valuable information. I have no problem consulting with others and sharing with them how I have achieved my various accomplishments. This is why I added "consulting" to the list of services I provide.

Some people that are not competing with you will be completely honest and tell you that they are following your steps because you inspired them. Take it as a compliment rather than a threat.

> *Inspiring others and helping others achieve their goals should be your mission.*

You aren't blessed with your gift and talents solely for your own enjoyment. Your gift and talents are given to you, so you may bless others. While they are busy trying to outshine you on your latest accomplishment you should be so focused on your vision while working on your next project, that you don't notice. If someone wants to expend energy on trying to keep up with you, rather than fulfilling their own vision, don't let it distract you. Stay focused! But if you believe someone has illegally stolen any aspect of your business model, seek legal counsel.

It is often difficult to identify a person who is competing with you or decide what to do once you discover this. Unfortunately, this is often the case with friends, people you have on your payroll, or someone that has a front seat to your life.

Signs that you have a competitor in your space are:

1. People that are often competing with those around them speak differently than those who are not. You might notice they often accuse others of being jealous or competing with them. You might hear them frequently use the word "hater". I am not referring to someone accusing one or two people of being jealous or competing, I'm referring to the habitual assumption that over time, multiple people are competing or jealous of them.

2. They tend to adopt every aspect of your life they see as desirable, while still accusing you of being the one competing.

3. They race to accomplish things with the expectation, assumption, and belief that others will be jealous once they accomplish the goal, rather than assuming others will be genuinely happy for them and no one will be jealous or upset. They mistake other people's tendency to be inspired by their accomplishments and success for jealousy.

4. They speak negatively about anyone who appears to have been given accolades or is recognized on the same playing field as them. It is as if other people's success negates and is a threat to theirs, and there isn't enough room for many people to succeed.

5. They have something to prove. Very often these are people that have been tremendously hurt in the past. They accomplish a lot of what they do in attempt to prove they are worthy or important. They may even continue to reiterate, re-post, or re-announce their significant moments of success in a repetitive manner to make sure everyone knows and remembers. You might notice specific times when these mentions or posts occur such as; when someone else accomplishes something, or when they become upset with someone.

6. They either get depressed, critical, or more competitive when someone else accomplishes something. You will see them switch gears when they get the news.

7. They are controlling! They try to control those close to them by preventing them from getting close to people they see as a threat or competition. They try to talk them out of endeavors or beneficial collaborations with others, because it isn't beneficial for them or may take them out of the number one spot in their life.

What do you do when you find out your friend, family member, coworker, or employee is in competition with you? Create some distance, so that you don't find yourself getting pulled into the race or the competition. If the relationship is toxic, unhealthy and detrimental to your emotional well-being, end it altogether. Remaining connected to people who are negative and pulling you into an ongoing competition will prevent productivity and interfere with your potential for happiness.

If you happen to be a person who struggles with competing and comparing, remember that others are usually inspired and motivated by you rather than competing or being jealous of you. It's very possible that the people you believe are jealous don't value the same things as you do, have a different definition of success, and have never looked at you as competition. Seeking help from a professional to determine why you relate to others this way and assume others perceive you this way, can be very helpful.

> *If your actions inspire others to dream more, learn more, do more, and become more, you are a leader.*
>
> *~ John Quincy Adams ~*

IV.

CHAPTER IV.
PEOPLE PLEASING

Many people have the tendency to navigate through life in a broken state while pretending to be whole. These same people have a habit of presenting a smile and doing kind acts for the world, while going home and failing to connect with or demonstrate affection to their own families. Such people are crying themselves to sleep at night, due to the stress of feeling inadequate and trying to keep up the façade. There are many seemingly happy, prosperous, and well-to-do people that are hurt, have low self-esteem, suffer from lack of confidence, and are feeling pretty hopeless. It is very easy to love the world and submit to its influence on our lives, but much more challenging to practice self-love or see ourselves as loveable, valuable, effective, or appreciated.

Due to such emptiness and self-doubt many of us get into the habit of feeling the need to please others, no matter the cost. Once you become a people pleaser, you are typically expected to be someone other than who you genuinely and authentically are.

When you exert more effort towards pleasing and gaining the approval of others rather than engaging in self-acceptance and contributing to your own happiness, you are setting yourself up for failure.

Going through life feeling like you don't measure up unless you gain approval from certain people or entities, promotes lack of fulfillment, frustration, stress, feelings of rejection, low self-esteem, exhaustion, depression, anxiety, and overall lack of happiness. Being a "people pleaser" never results in your own happiness, in fact, it is a major contributing factor to feelings of sadness and failure.

How do you know if you are a habitual people pleaser? If you find yourself asking the following questions too often, you have fallen into the dark hole of people pleasing.

What will they think?

What if they don't want to talk to me anymore after I say no?

What if they get mad at me?

People who live to please others, love to feel as if they are liked, approved of, and accepted by others. This can be truly crippling and even result in depression, if they feel rejected, have failed friendships, or when someone is less than pleased with them. It is important to understand that if there isn't one single person in the world who dislikes you, then you are probably not doing something right. Perhaps you are hiding the real you, and you are indeed a people pleaser. This is not to say you should strive for or enjoy when others dislike you, however you have to get comfortable with the idea that some people will love you, and some will not. You will not be everyone's cup of tea.

> *A friend to all is a friend to none.*
>
> *~ Aristotle ~*

It is 100% impossible to be both a people pleaser and an authentic person at the same time. Accepting that some people will criticize you when you aren't doing your best, then envy you when you are accomplishing great things, is important when trying to kick the people pleasing habit. Some people are not going to like you whether you are winning or losing.

> *If you struggle with the need to feel accepted*
> *or liked by everyone, today should be the day*
> *you begin working toward learning*
> *why you struggle in this area*
> *and start changing your mindset.*

Unfortunately some people won't support you because they don't believe you are capable of landing your dream job, getting a promotion, starting your own business, choosing a good mate, writing a book, or being an effective and impactful leader. If this treatment comes from family members this might hurt more than any rejection from outside sources. Many people have a narrow view of what success looks like and what it takes to achieve it.

In most families the standard expectation is going to college, getting your degree, and remaining at the same job for forty years until you retire with a set amount of monthly retirement income. For many THAT IS SUCCESS!

> *A word of encouragement during moments of failure*
> *is worth more than hours of praise*
> *during moments of success.*

You need friends and family members on your side during the challenging times on the ground floor, because starting a business, starting a family, completing college, or starting your career are all quite difficult. If it were easy, everyone would be doing it.

In conclusion, I recommend getting prepared for people you believe care about you, to show their lack of belief in your ability to soar beyond their safe version of success. Remain passionate about the work that you do every day, and remember it will never be suitable for, applauded by, or make sense to everyone else. Remember that you are living a life of purpose, and that your journey was meant just for you. In addition, being careful about hurting other people's feelings is not the same as people pleasing. Many of us refrain from being harsh, abrasive or hurtful with our words and actions. On the other hand, some say and do whatever they want, when they want it, and however they want it. This is mainly due to individual's personality, upbringing, and the level of compassion for the feelings of others.

V.

Chapter V.
Steps toward change

The first step in changing your mindset from feeling the need to please people rather than doing and saying what truly makes you happy, is understanding that there are some people who will never be happy with you no matter how many Yes's you give, and there are some people who will never stop liking you or supporting you, no matter how many No's you give. For example, when someone attempts to engage you in projects, events, or assignments that you simply can't fit into your schedule due to time, energy, or interest, they won't take it personally.

> *People that genuinely love you*
> *will feel the same about you whether you are able*
> *to give them what they want or not.*

They will love, support, and encourage you whether you are at your best or worst. They will support you when you need support, encourage you when you need encouragement, give constructive criticism when necessary, and be genuinely happy for you when you succeed. They will be there when you are just starting out, telling you not to quit because you ran into a few obstacles or made a mistake. These same people will still be there once you have mastered your craft and have become one of the best in your field.

Don't become angry or resentful of the people that didn't support you from the beginning or shut you off when they couldn't control you. Perhaps they began to dislike you once they learned you had to put your time and energy towards your own endeavors and projects, before you could help them complete or build theirs. Once the people that were afraid to support you while being afraid to put their reputation on the line finally see that you have made it and decide you are now worthy of their public support, don't become bitter. Simply hug them and say, "Thank you." You don't have to keep them abreast of what is happening in your career or what engagements you have going on, nor do you have to maintain a relationship with them. If they didn't care enough to lift you up and show support when you were just getting started, in your darkest hour, or thought you might ruin their "so-called" reputation if they publicly supported you, then don't uplift their reputation for them by being publicly associated with them once you have succeeded. You can love them, hug them, and wish them the best without letting them in on your success, since they failed to be there during the failures you endured.

> *If you live for acceptance*
> *you will die from rejection.*

People pleasing hides the real you and puts you in a position where you feel you can't be authentic. When you aren't authentic it is hard for others to trust you, understand you, and unfortunately it is also hard for others to like you. I had to learn this the hard way. I have been in personal and business relationships and friendships that I desperately wanted to work out. Because I wanted those relationships to work, I refrained from being who I authentically am. There were times when I was offended, my feelings were hurt, or I became upset by the actions of others, however I refrained from speaking up. For most of my life I had been able to communicate my disapproval of the actions of others when necessary. However, during moments or throughout personal and business relationships in which I chose to be passive and not express my thoughts or feelings, it harmed the relationship more than helped it. My choice to "keep everything inside" resulted in others viewing me as confusing and created resentment. When I finally released my thoughts, they came out more aggressively because they were suppressed and prolonged. If you have held your true feelings in for six months and allowed several small offenses to build-up, when you finally express them several months later, they will come out more harshly than if you had communicated them in a timely fashion or at the actual time of the offense. At this point, you have a build-up of resentment, anger, hurt feelings, and old wounds. If you fail to communicate your authentic position on any issue or with any person that is important to you at the appropriate time, they will believe your sudden, yet delayed outburst is coming out of left field. They will feel as though you have misled them, are attacking them over something minor or insignificant, and that you have a personal issue with them.

> *When you don't like yourself and are a people pleaser,*
> *you might find yourself chasing after people.*

You have an idea of the type of people you want in your life, and you'll find yourself actively seeking out that type of person. The problem with this tendency is that once you achieve these relationships and friendships, you end up getting your feelings hurt. Somehow, they let you down and you end up disappointed, eventually losing these relationships altogether. The reason for this outcome is that you entered the relationship based on an intention to benefit from these relationships, rather than the actual connection and genuineness.

It is true that you can't take everyone with you as you move forward to the next phase of life or success, and some people will choose not to walk along-side you into that phase for various reasons.

> *If you find that everyone you get close to*
> *or develop a relationship with*
> *is either walking away or you have to cut them off,*
> *you should look in the mirror*
> *and do some self-evaluating.*

Sometimes we are arrogant, self-righteous, condescending, demeaning, judgmental, controlling, or even outright immature. Unfortunately, once we have reached this stage of ridiculousness we often don't acknowledge our flaws, we blame others for failed relationships, and convince ourselves that our way of thinking and behaving is the right way. If several of your family members, leaders, staff, or friends have left you for similar reasons, please stop, take a moment and self-evaluate. Self-examination will allow you to end the dysfunctional and harmful behavior that continues to push everyone you care about, out of your life.

There is such a thing as a people pleaser, and then there is a people chaser. Chasing people is another downfall for people seeking success. When you seek out people whom you believe can contribute to your success and that is all the relationship is built on, you are setting yourself up for a disaster, people walking in and out of your life, and turmoil. I have witnessed people working hard to be in the presence and in the likes of others to the extent that they appeared desperate, and thirsty. I strongly believe having a hunger for success and beneficial relationships is great and should be important to one who is pursuing a life of success, however desperation is not a good look.

> *When we seek the company of individuals*
> *more or equal to our desire to be*
> *in the presence of God, it is unhealthy.*

You put yourself in a position in which you have no power or influence while in the presence of these persons that you so aggressively pursued. You find yourself constantly trying to prove yourself to them, and will more than likely never feel you measure up in their presence. Refrain from placing men on a pedestal. In most cases they aren't as perfect as you think they are. You will eventually find yourself disappointed when you learn they aren't who you envisioned from afar. Many people that go through life pursuing the next important or successful friend, partner, spouse, or relationship of any kind, find themselves moving from friend to friend, partner to partner, or relationship to relationship. They are chasing something that is false, rather than deciding what they want and trusting that the right people will be placed right in front of them. As a result, they end up getting hurt, pushed away, or disappointed.

I can't count the number of times I thought someone was successful based on what they were driving, wearing, the way they spoke, behaved, how popular they were, who they were related to, and even where they lived. Somehow unintentionally I found out their home was like something out of an episode of hoarders. A few of them lived in substandard housing, didn't own anything of real value, didn't make enough money to afford the material items they possessed, their relationships were unhealthy, and their home life was dysfunctional.

> *Get involved with people for the right reasons*
> *rather than who they appear to be or appear to have.*
> *Don't judge a book by its cover.*

Once I reach the final destination of my journey to success, I would like to look around and not feel that everyone next to me feels like I owe them something, or I am successful because of their efforts.

A good example of this type of judgment is the decision to marry for money. I would rather marry and build a life of success with the man of my dreams, have an authentic marriage, actually love the person I am with for who they are not what they can provide for me, and be truly happy and genuine, than to marry someone who I would never have been attracted to had it not been for their success. Marrying someone just for their money would be quite unfulfilling for me, because the foundation of the relationship would be built on things that can't sustain a marriage. Money can't buy happiness, love, or genuineness. Status and wealth can be built with the right person, but genuine love, trust, honesty, and happiness also have to be acquired with the right person. Although status and wealth can significantly increase the likelihood of a better life, a person's money, status, fame, and power does not guarantee good health, happiness, or an improved quality of life.

> *Base your personal and business relationships*
> *first on internal qualities,*
> *followed by external ones.*

In relationships built on financial status many people initially believe they have based their connection on the proper principles, until they are knee deep in realization that they don't truly know the person outside of their wealth and influence. This is not always problematic, since a major component of relationships is remaining committed to getting to know each other and growing together on an ongoing basis.

Not all business or personal relationships that are initiated based on finances, wealth, or status end due to conflict or unfavorable circumstances. These relationships like any other relationship have the ability to grow and become healthy and successful. All parties involved must remain committed to completing the work required for growth.

CHAPTER VI.

FEAR, FAILURE, AND REJECTION ARE COUSINS

Perfection is unrealistic. One of the main reasons we dislike ourselves is because we aren't perfect. This is especially true for women. Somehow many of us see imperfection as failure. For example, we can be a size six, 23% body fat, and a BMI of 24, but are still unhappy and ashamed of our body. This means we have completely disregarded the fact that many women would love to have those numbers, that we are unhappy with. Instead, we should be celebrating the fact that we are very close to where we want to be, and just may be in need a few minor changes to achieve our weight loss and fitness goals. We tend to focus on what we are lacking, rather than our strengths. This typically slows down progress, may completely ruin results already achieved due to stress, and could impede our potential for future growth.

Goals, desires, and dreams that you fear and view as unattainable are only unattainable because you have told yourself so. What happens when you decide to push past your fears and your efforts result in failure? Failure often results in feelings of inadequacy. If we aren't careful, failure will push many of us back into a state of crippling fear. Often times when we fail, we decide that the possibility of success isn't worth the risk of failure. This is mainly because failure is heavy, painful, and creates a sense of defeat. Many people choose not to experience that same heaviness and pain repetitively, which means they stop trying.

Rejection and failure are part of life, especially in our careers, relationships, business ownership, and in leadership. You will not accomplish much in life, if you allow fear of rejection and failure deter you from taking risks. Most major life accomplishments involve a wide array of risks such as risk of financial loss, deterioration in family dynamics, failed relationships, exhaustion, and more. Essentially, if you have no experience with failure, you have not taken any major risks and probably haven't accomplished very much.

> *You must be willing to take risks, face rejection,*
> *accept failure, and bounce back after a fall*
> *in order to gain and maintain confidence, move forward,*
> *continue creating, and ultimately succeed.*

PART II:

GETTING DOWN TO BUSINESS

VII.

Chapter VII.

Discovering Your Gift

Our Life's journey is the longest and most important journey we will ever embark upon. Navigate through this journey with clear intention and direction. It's time to decide where you are going in life, why you are going in that direction, and how you will get there. Let's discuss the basics of getting started.

I purposely put discovering your gift and purpose first in the business part of this book, because they both play a key role in deciding what career path you should take, or what type of business you could succeed at. Your gift is an ability that comes naturally to you, you are good at it, can do it effortlessly, and would probably do it for free, if you didn't have bills to pay. Your purpose is connected to the reason you were born, and why you are present on earth.

> *What were you born to do?*
> *Your gift and purpose are connected.*

Once you discover, learn and take the proper steps utilizing both to create happiness in your daily life, it can result in a fulfilling career and a rewarding life. You can have many talents, but only one gift. Your many talents will enhance your gift and help carry out and live in your purpose.

Talents are simply things you are good at. For example, my talents are counseling, coaching, fitness training, specialized nutrition advice, writing, and developing business. These talents are all useful for utilizing my gift, which is helping others. I help others through coaching, counseling, training, writing, and through my businesses. My purpose or the reason I was born, is to help others transform their lives in all areas of body, mind, and spirit.

> *The moment in which you discover*
> *exactly what you were born to do,*
> *is a pretty emotional and memorable moment.*

My moment of discovery was what most people consider an "Aha" moment.

While identifying personal and professional deficits and weaknesses is an important part of becoming a great leader, professional, or business owner, you must also identify your purpose, your gifts and talents, and your strengths.

Prior to opening a business or embarking on any new endeavor, get a pad of paper and a pen and write down the answers to the following questions:

Who am I, and what is my purpose in life?

What was I born to do?

What are my gifts, what am I good at?

What do I want in the areas of family, career, health, wealth, and personal growth?

What do I need to do to achieve and acquire the things I want?

How can I use my gifts, skills, strengths, and experiences to walk in my purpose?

What am I less good at, and what can I do to improve in this area?

Do I need to develop and advance in these weak areas in order to achieve my goals?

Who can I reach out to for help with growth and development in these areas?

What sacrifices will I have to make to accomplish my goals?

What is a reasonable timeline for accomplishing these goals?

Answering these questions will give you a starting point for developing a blue print for the path you should take to owning your business, starting your brand, walking in your purpose, and living the life that was meant just for you. I asked myself these questions in the beginning, yet I still made several mistakes. Some of those mistakes were huge and costly. Other costs and sacrifices include: unnecessary stress, sleepless nights, relationships, friendships, financial strain and blows to my credit history, fatigue, tears, low mood, reduced vacation time, social life, and more. I would love to help you prevent some of these same costly mistakes.

1. Discover your gift - that thing you do naturally with very little effort

2. Discover your purpose - what are you supposed to use the gift for

3. Strategically develop a plan and write it down

4. Assess and determine necessary resources, time, and tools to accomplish the plan

5. Prioritize tasks on your plan and set up a timeline

6. Seek professional help to ensure your plan is solid and ready to be initiated, or consider professional advice and make necessary revisions to your plan

7. Initiate the plan

8. Continue to seek help and professional advice to ensure your steps and work are professional, legal, and ethical

9. Don't let work take over your life

10. Receive professional evaluation and critique prior to revealing finished work

These 10 steps sound simple, however there is a lot of work involved with each step. This will be very challenging and time consuming, but you are more than capable of moving forward, and putting your business plan in place.

HOW I DISCOVERED MY PURPOSE

I was a Licensed Clinical Professional Counselor when I discovered my passion for fitness. Sure, I loved running and exercising in my spare time, but didn't realize I enjoyed helping other people start their fitness journey, achieve their fitness goals, and have an empowering impact on their healthy lifestyle journey, until I reached my early 30's. Many people watched me transform my body after gaining several pounds with both of my pregnancies in my 20's and were inspired to do the same. Eventually, I put my counseling career on hold to open a fitness center so that I could share my passion, help others achieve the same results, and carry out my lifetime dream of being a business owner. At this point I had a son getting ready to enter middle school, and a daughter in high school. Although there were challenges, failures and victories that came with the success during the first two years of business ownership, we were able to get our fitness center to the point of being fully staffed and pretty much self-sufficient. I was pleased that this finally allowed me to have the opportunity and return to my true career of counseling for which I had attended college, became licensed, and spent many years developing and sharpening my skills prior to starting my therapy practice. I applied for and was offered a full-time therapist position with two different companies and remained at each of them for about thirty days. I'd never remained with a company less than four years since officially starting my career 20 years ago. It was impossible to focus on my career with a new company and learn my job, as I was more interested in what was going on at my wellness and fitness business throughout the day. I very quickly decided that my being distracted on the job and primarily focused on my place of business wasn't fair to the company that hired me or the clients I was working with. To be honest, I was ecstatic about getting hired with one of the companies due to their reputation and constant growth, up until the very first day when I pulled into the parking lot and reported for my first day of work.

MY AHA! MOMENT

As soon as I put my black Dodge in park, a profound feeling of displacement came over me. The excitement I had prior to that moment instantaneously disappeared, and it was as if I heard a voice say, "What are you doing? You are not supposed to be here! I have given you your own business and platform, and that is where you should be."

I'd heard this voice before and knew it very well. Since I had already negotiated my salary and accepted the job, I decided to report to work anyway. After a few short weeks I told my supervisor that I felt horrible, but I couldn't stay due to my attention and energy invested in my own business. I declared that I only wanted to work for their company if I were able to be 100% committed. Needless to say, I left shortly after to return to the platform I was blessed with and assigned to.

YOUR ASSIGNMENT IS CHOSEN BY GOD AND DISCOVERED BY YOU

Once I returned home, the same voice that spoke to me in the parking lot had another message for me. This time the message I received was:

"I blessed you with all the tools for this very moment more than a decade ago, when I conveniently set up an environment for you to work in a management position. You were earning a good salary and received supervision for your clinical license at the same time. Back then, I made it convenient and possible for you to earn your clinical license, because I knew you would need it for private practice today."

This was a revelatory moment for me because I remembered saying about thirteen years prior, that I was getting licensed so that I could have my own counseling practice. The strange thing was I never really thought too much about private practice after receiving my license, never pursued or looked into it, and always applied for jobs in my field with other companies. Even more odd was the fact that I had the desire to open a fitness center prior to opening my counseling practice, even though I had been a counselor much longer, than was a fitness professional. I had never really thought too much about either of these facts until this moment.

I realized that my ultimate goal was always to go into private practice, but I hadn't made any effort to pursue private practice up until this point because apparently, I wasn't meant to until now. I found it strange that at this juncture I had no choice but to open my own practice, since I was already a business owner and needed to maintain control over my schedule. It was as if I was thrust or thrown into the position I was meant to be in. Everything I had been working on and achieving over the previous 15 years lead up to, prepared me for, and was destined into play at this very moment. The key to making the best choices in this matter was determining whether I would listen to the voice that was guiding me. Some would say this voice was my intuition or instincts, but I believe it was God leading me into my life's purpose. Would I believe owning two businesses was absurd, risky, and not possible, or would I do my research, develop a plan and dive into my next business venture as instructed?

After being invited to open a practice and share office space with another therapist, I realized how natural this choice and process was for me. I didn't hesitate very much as I knew I would open a practice at some point, which was why I acquired the clinical license in the first place. The transition was smooth, seamless, and involved very little stress. Compared to opening a fitness center it was also relatively inexpensive. Once I opened my counseling practice and began spending time seeing clients at the office, while still training a few clients at the gym, I noticed some very significant similarities. I observed that I was discussing how to overcome mental barriers in the way of living a healthy lifestyle with my clients at the gym. I was counseling clients and members on relationship problems that were interfering with their ability to remain consistent with training and eating healthy. I was also coaching them on financial difficulties and how to make sure they were able to afford to purchase the right foods and maintain their training packages. Finally, I encouraged them to reflect on their old patterns of depression or anxiety prior to starting a regular fitness regimen and living a healthy lifestyle. Many of them were able to recognize the connection between living a healthy lifestyle and improved mental health. Hence the importance of managing their finances in a way that allowed them to continue our training programs. In addition, I found that quite often, I was incorporating physical activity and nutritional changes into many of my client's treatment goals in order to promote improved sleeping habits, increase energy levels, and help manage symptoms.

As a result of ongoing coaching and counseling many of my clients, I learned that an individual's personal life such as problems at home, at work, financial distress, feeling purposeless, lack of self-esteem, and sense of connection to others, was strongly related to whether they succeeded at maintaining a regular fitness regimen, establishing healthy long-term eating habits, and achieving their weight loss or fitness goals. Assessing clients as they enrolled in programs at the gym, or engaged in counseling at the office, and observing and documenting their changes and success over time, more than confirmed this correlation. We had several members and clients that were doing well, losing weight, building muscle, and feeling great until life happened. A challenge or change in their personal life such as loss of a family member, a child leaving for college, a pregnancy, marital or relationship problems, other familial issues and relationships, financial difficulties, or lack of confidence or self-esteem, significantly impacted their ability to remain consistent at living a healthy lifestyle. This is when I realized we had to help our members deal with the things that were going on in their personal lives outside of the gym, if we wanted to help them achieve their fitness goals and live a healthy lifestyle. It just so happens, we have a licensed counselor on staff at the gym to provide help with those things! I discovered that my purpose was not just to be a counselor or a trainer. If that were the case I wouldn't need to own a fitness center or a private counseling practice of my own. I could have worked at any mental health agency or fitness center and provided those services to my clients. I recognized that my purpose was to help individuals, families, and groups of individuals improve their overall quality of life. I wasn't supposed to just help a client improve their mental health and interpersonal relationships. I wasn't supposed to just help my clients achieve their fitness goals, I am supposed to help each person I serve achieve success in five core areas of life! This is when our program *Your Exhilarating Life* was born.

Your Exhilarating Life is a life transformation program that was created to help our clients address these five core areas of life in order to achieve happiness, success, improved health, set goals, and attain their goals in every area of life. These five core areas are:

Family and interpersonal relationships

Self-esteem and confidence

Business and career

Mental Health and emotional well-being

Fitness and nutrition

I truly am grateful that I listened to "the voice", put in the work, and maintained endurance to see the vision through. I had confidence in myself and lacked fear of unchartered territory. I honestly didn't know anyone who had done this. Although I have met many since starting, I honestly didn't know anyone personally who had opened a business starting from scratch. As I reflect upon my journey, it surprises me that I was so courageous and unafraid.

CHAPTER VIII.

BUSINESS AND CAREER

WRITE THE VISION AND MAKE IT CRYSTAL CLEAR

Develop a plan and write it down. I can't stress enough the importance of writing. As I continue telling my clients, members, and enrollees, I still have my original notebook paper on which I began writing the initial thoughts for *Club Exhilaration*. I noted numerous possible names, programs, and services to be provided. Today, when I stumble across those pages with my barely legible handwritten notes, I am amazed and in awe that an entire business started with chicken scratch on a piece of paper and evolved into an organized company with several members, staff, equipment, and business partners. Of course, it started out with notes on paper and evolved into a formal business plan, contractual agreements, construction, banking and financial agreements, building permits, and everything else that comes with starting a business. However, the initial thoughts of my business were simple moments of brainstorming with a pad of paper and an ink pen.

> *Having an organized business plan provides vision and structure for your future company.*

It forces you to think rationally, realistically, and objectively about your enterprise. A business plan also makes it easier to communicate goals, objectives, and strategies to future investors, supporters, and employees. Please ensure you have a thorough and professional business plan prior to asking lenders for money or realtors for office space or a building. There are numerous resources available online, if you need help developing a business plan. Hiring a business consultant or a business coach is a great idea. It is important that you check individual's or company's experience and credentials prior to hiring them. Don't rely on their word that they have helped others. Do your research and seek out testimonials from legitimate and thriving businesses that give them credit for assisting them in making their business and dream a reality.

> *Write the vision and make it plain on tablets*
> *so whoever reads it can run to tell others.*
> *It is not yet time for the message to come true, but that*
> *time is coming soon; the message will come true. It may*
> *seem like a long time but be patient and wait for it*
> *because it will surely come; it will not be delayed.*
>
> *~ Habakkuk 2:2-3~*

Failure to set a timeline may result in slow progress, no progress, missed steps in the process, additional fees due to poor planning, or lack of direction. There are several steps that need to take place prior to your grand opening so staying on task is critical.

RESOURCES

Each business requires a different set or list of resources in order to help initiate and carry out the business plan. Some of those resources are financial such as lenders and investors, some are contractors for various services and products, entities that provide necessary licenses and certifications, and others are mentors, and individual advisors. It is important to ascertain and list the resources that will be required for your business during the planning process, rather than waiting until you are close to your grand opening.

Your City's Business Development and Planning department is a good place to start. Give them a call, advise them of your intentions to open a business, and ask for a list of required certifications, licenses, inspections, and documents that must be acquired prior to opening.

A business mentor is a great asset and will help you consider all aspects of your project. You may need to consult a realtor depending on the type of space you require for your enterprise. A good realtor can help get the best bang for your buck when choosing a location. There are numerous other professionals that you might find helpful depending on the type of business you plan to open, such as an attorney that specializes in business law, a business Manager, if you don't plan to manage yourself, and an accountant.

As you are starting, building, or running your business, you might hear the following clichés:

Don't let anyone outwork you.
No one should be working harder at your business than you.

There is a lot of truth to these two statements however, at some point you must transition from worker to boss. In most small "mom and pop" businesses the owner is there throughout most of the day, has very few staff members, and typically can't afford to hire very many employees. Most large corporations have owners who were present during the building phase, initial grand opening, and possibly the first few years. Once the business is running smoothly, efficiently, and in a productive manner, they become less involved with day to day operations, as they have put proper staff in place.

Owners of large corporations typically move on to other business ventures within the company or start new companies altogether once daily operations are in order. This allows them to create multiple streams of revenue. At that point, they keep tabs on expense and revenue reports, remain in touch with financial officers, board members, and key employees they have hired, and make regular appearances on site. If you are the owner and are working from sunrise to sunset indefinitely, you are not doing something right. There will be days and sometimes months when you have special projects, tours, launches, and releases in which you will work around the clock.

> *Ideally you should have moved beyond the point*
> *in which you are still working around the clock*
> *for all 52 weeks of a year, beyond the seven year mark*
> *after opening your business.*

If this is the case you might want to consult with other business owners or your mentor, to figure out what you are doing wrong. Personally, I didn't become self-employed so that I could work 20 hours a day for the rest of my life. For the first couple of years I worked such extensive hours, and most nights I continue to work late on my computer at home. Although I still work from home when away from the office, I am no longer married to the walls of my business from 5 am until 10 pm.

This was a major milestone in my business for me. As an owner I don't have the "hardest worker" mentality. I have more of a "smartest worker" mentality. Although I started out with the intentions and habit of being the first one in the building in the morning and the last one to leave at night, that is no longer a goal for me. I have done that before and I literally had no social life, very little rest, very little time to spend with my family, and I must say I enjoyed it because I take pride in being a business owner. Eventually I grew tired, and realized I was allowing other areas of my life to deteriorate while I was at work for 12-15 hours a day.

I changed my approach and found out how to get more done in a shorter period of time. I explored how I could fit paid staff into the budget, what systems or people I could put into place that would allow me to spend more time at home, and how I could safely and confidently ensure our business was secure and running smoothly in my absence. My goal was to focus on productivity rather than length of time on site. I learned that maximizing your time is the smartest way to work. Working fifteen hour days is great if you have absolutely nothing else to do, don't have a family at home, or other obligations and responsibilities.

> *The number of hours you spend on the clock*
> *isn't as important as what you accomplish*
> *while you are on the clock.*

It is very helpful to have a daily task list and schedule out your day, hour by hour. This helps to stay on course. In today's society you could easily end up spending two hours of your eight-hour day on social media. If you tend to do that throughout your workday, I encourage you to schedule that activity just as you would other things. Once you schedule the time you will spend on social media, don't allow yourself to log-on until your schedule says it is time to do so. This will help ensure your day is productive.

Below is an example of an eight-hour schedule. This is useful regardless of whether you work for yourself or not. Depending on the nature of your business, this schedule may not be ideal and it is simply an example. On some days I see between eight to ten clients. My schedule is similar on my long days, just longer hours and less time for paperwork. This schedule would be more suitable for days on which I see fewer clients and can catch up on paperwork.

8:00 Check email, review task list, check voicemail, respond to messages
9:00 Session scheduled
10:00 Session scheduled
11:00 Check social media and text messages
11:30 - 1pm Paperwork, notes, check email, follow-up calls and emails
1:00 Lunch
2:00 Session scheduled
3:00 Meeting scheduled
4:00 Complete documentation and paperwork
4:30 Go home

IX.

CHAPTER IX.

FAITH, RISK, HARD WORK, AND SACRIFICE

Choose a business that is connected to your purpose and provides a product or service that a large portion of the population needs. This will greatly increase your chances of success. Selecting a business that only a small handful of people need, will put you at risk of losing money and restricting your potential for profit and success.

Choose a business that ensures you will earn revenue while you sleep. If your business requires you to go door to door every day in order to make money, you might want to reevaluate whether you will have the time and endurance to maintain that level of physical exertion each day.

> *You need a business in which customers, clients,*
> *or members will invest on an ongoing basis.*

They will come to you for services or products versus you going to them, their lives will be improved as a result of your business or services, and a significant portion of the population will need or want your service. Clients and customers "coming to you" simply means they are seeking you out. For example, my clients in therapy typically contact their insurance company asking for a professional in their area. The insurance company will provide them with names, addresses, and phone numbers of the clinicians they have listed in network in their area. If most people will not want or need the products or services you are offering more than once, you have to determine if that one-time investment from each customer will be beneficial and profitable enough to justify investing in this product or service.

When you have decided to open a business, vision is very important. You have to be able to see the successful enterprise before you get there, rather than afterwards. Coming up with an idea that lacks vision is a recipe for disaster. If all you have is an idea, you will not have the passion and motivation needed when or if your journey becomes difficult. Vision will help you remain motivated and maintain endurance when things aren't going as planned, when you are fatigued, or when you are faced with adversity. Business ownership requires faith, sacrifice, hard work, and risk.

FAITH

Faith is the opposite of fear, and means you are totally relying on God or something bigger than yourself for an outcome. If you work hard, but lack faith, you reduce the chances of total success. In addition, you have to pair hard work with that faith, because your successful business isn't going to manifest without the necessary hard work. You have to put in the necessary work, and have faith that the work you have done and the seeds you have planted will produce the harvest you desire.

SACRIFICE

Many of us have strong faith and work very hard, but lack the required endurance and discipline for the task at hand. Most of us also fail to understand the sacrifices that must be made in order to succeed. Understand that sacrifice isn't just about giving up basic things, like a few extra dollars or an occasional night out. Sacrifices that we make as we are on our journey to achieve our best life, are sometimes sacrifices that you never imagined you would have to make.

> *Definition of Sacrifice:*
> *~ destruction or surrender of something*
> *for the sake of something else ~*

We have to make sacrifices for everything that matters to us in our lives. We make sacrifices for our children, spouses, personal gain or well-being, our careers, businesses, families, and our friends. Some of those sacrifices are very difficult, some are quite painful, and others you may barely notice. Some of those sacrifices you may regret later on, so be careful about what you give up today to get what you want tomorrow. I encourage you to ask yourself the following questions.

1. **What are you willing to give up or sacrifice for what you want?**
2. **Is the thing you want worth that sacrifice?**
3. **What are the chances that you will regret making those sacrifices later on?**
4. **What are the chances you will regret NOT making those sacrifices down the road?**

If you find that what or who you are sacrificing is not worth that thing you are gaining, setting new goals or taking a new route might not be a bad idea. Don't sacrifice the things that are permanent, positive, and healthy for things that are temporary.

For example, neglecting your personal physical or mental health, neglecting or throwing away all of your close lifetime friendships for friendships with people you barely know, because you think they can help you achieve that dream, and allowing your family to deteriorate and fall apart while you are out pursuing goals and dreams, are all very risky sacrifices. Once you have neglected your family for an extended period of time while pursuing life goals and your career, it is highly likely that your family will no longer be intact, once you have finally succeeded at your desired accomplishments.

If you have failed to care for yourself physically and emotionally, it is highly likely your physical and mental health will have deteriorated over time. In this case, it is possible that some of the damage is irreversible, depending on the severity of the destruction. This might not be a sacrifice that you can return to later and pick up where you left off, so be very careful about what you are giving up or leaving behind.

RISK

I left a Masters level State job with great benefits, a promising retirement and stability in order to work for myself. Some people thought this was a poor and risky decision. I agreed with my naysayers in that this was a huge risk. Not only was this decision a risk, it was also a sacrifice that required great faith in order to walk in my purpose. I temporarily sacrificed ongoing financial stability, since I would no longer have my paycheck every two weeks. I also sacrificed affordable dental and medical insurance for my family. As a State employee, medical benefits were very inexpensive. These sacrifices were huge! I had to decide if these sacrifices would be worth the things I was pursuing in the long run. My logic then and still now is that everything we do in life that is significant, life changing, and epic involves risk, sacrifices, and faith. I wasn't in the habit or mood to play safe, and felt very confident in taking this risk. I was confident that if for some reason I failed, I would still have my education and years of experience to fall back on. I could always go back and apply for jobs, if I needed to. My willingness to take this huge risk was a direct result of the level of faith that I had in God and the confidence I had in myself. I decided that I was no longer going to remain afraid to pursue my goals and dreams, walk in my purpose, or refrain from being the person I was meant to be. After having been employed full-time with benefits for 14 years, I decided to leave the safe zone and jump. For the first time in my adult life I didn't have to clock-in or clock-out, I didn't have a retirement package, I didn't have company health or dental insurance, and I no longer had what most Americans consider security. I also no longer had a regular or consistent paycheck. For these reasons, I worked harder than I had ever before in my entire life.

While stepping out on faith, there are more sacrifices than you can imagine. I knew there would be sacrifices, but I had no idea how extensive they would be, until I was waist deep in them. A few of the most challenging sacrifices made during the first few years of business ownership outside of the ones previously mentioned were family time, sleep, and financial freedom. Family time was a major sacrifice, because you are literally working from sunrise to sunset, depending on the nature of your business. Most nights I would come home and power up my laptop to do more work after already working a 12-15 hour day. Financial freedom is sacrificed due to the large initial investment you put into your business. Supplies, equipment, utilities, rent, signage, licenses, certifications, inspections, and permits can rapidly catapult you into the red or a financial deficit. It can take quite a while to recover from such costs.

For most businesses it takes three to five years to recover from initial investment, before seeing a surplus.

Sleep is sacrificed mainly due to long work hours, and sometimes anxiety, accompanied by worry. If your business is experiencing a financial deficit, you might find that you are at times uneasy or on edge which can interrupt your sleep pattern.

By the second year of business ownership we started to experience some financial strain. We believe it is important to share these challenging times with our audience and readers because this is part of the process for many new business owners. Business owners making a substantial initial investment, have paid staff, utilities, supplies, etc. are more likely to experience such financial turbulence rather than individuals with web based businesses. Most businesses just like most marriages don't make it beyond the first few years. This is because after the honeymoon phase and all of the initial excitement is over things can become a bit rocky.

> *Success does not happen overnight, it is progressive.*

You have made huge sacrifices that you never thought you could or would, and you work harder than you ever imagined in order to make it happen. I must admit that there were plenty of days on which I considered quitting and going back to a 9-5 where it was safe and fewer risks. Business ownership was tough, but I continued to remind myself that these tough times were necessary sacrifices and a part of the process.

> *You can't open a business and get lazy.*
> *Business ownership is similar to a marriage,*
> *therefore the real work starts after the honeymoon.*

Getting your business open is only half the battle, just as remaining happy beyond the first couple of blissful years in marriage prior to experiencing any real life problems is only half the battle. After you have your grand opening the real faith, work, sacrifice, and risks take place. Prior to becoming a business owner, I had always worked hard. I had completed two college degrees, a clinical license that took two years of postgraduate school to acquire, had been married for well over a decade, was a parent, and a full-time professional in my field of study for more than fifteen years.

Although we had all of these experiences and accomplishments under our belt, none of them quite prepared us for the challenges of business ownership. Seemingly we had already worked harder than we ever would, and business ownership would allow freedom, more time with family, more time to relax, and flexibility. This couldn't be further from the truth!

After opening our first business we worked harder, more hours, had less free time, less time to spend with family, less flexibility, and less freedom than ever! Being aware that this was only temporary, helped us maintain endurance to open other businesses. We had faith that the time, work, energy, and dedication we were putting into our businesses would eventually result in freedom, more time with family, flexibility, and overall control of our daily schedule.

> *Because we had faith, took the risks, did the work, and made the sacrifices, we are still in business and still continue to grow.*

73

STRIVE TO BE A BUSINESS OWNER
RATHER THAN A HUSTLER

Many people start a hustle and call it a business. When you decide to start a business, please make sure you understand the difference between a hustle and a legitimate and verifiable business. There are so many hustles out there, that people tend to create or get involved with to make extra cash. There is nothing wrong with a hustle as long as it is legal, just make sure you aren't getting confused and mistaking it for a business.

If you look up the definition of hustling, it is often defined as involving deception and "shady" business. Are you running a legitimate business, or do you have a hustle? Some of the signs that you might be running a hustle rather than a business are no investment, you can't legally promote the business, you have to keep certain aspects of the business hidden or removed from the public eye, selling random items with no Tax ID or business license, getting paid "under the table" and avoiding taxes, or partaking in any deceptive practices to initiate or carry out the services, are indications that you have a hustle rather than a business. If your business can be shut down or taken from you any day by entities such as law enforcement, or the government due to noncompliance, illegal, or unethical business practices, you have a hustle. If you are a legitimate business owner, you should consider changing your language when referring to your businesses or business practices. Instead of suggesting you are hustling, be a professional and proclaim you are working long hours, building relationships, connecting with the right people, engaging in professional development, setting new goals, challenging yourself, and getting better every day, rather than hustling. That is a more professional way of describing your hard work.

If you are a legitimate business, you should have basic things like business cards, a website, and business hours. Anytime someone approaches me with a sales pitch or they are trying to offer a service or product to me, I always ask for a business card and a website. If they don't have business cards and a website in this day and age, that tells me they are running a hustle rather than a legitimate business. I repeat, you are not a legitimate business and your business lacks professionalism without these basic and essential components.

> *It is very important to communicate your experience and expertise to potential clients.*

One way to accomplish this is to ask all clients or customers you have worked with, to rate you on google and your social media pages, so that your potential clients or customers are able to see that you are legitimate, provide quality products and services, and have professional experience. Most clients don't want to be your guinea pig. If they are your first client, or if they can't verify that you have actually been successful at what you are offering them, it will be difficult for them to trust you. When I first started my fitness training business, I ran small boot camps in the basement of my home and at local parks for free. I tracked each participant's progress, took before and after pictures, and made sure I had something to support my claims that I can help people transform their bodies. Regardless of the type of business you have, you can always ask customers for written testimonials to include on your website.

If you do not have business hours, it should be obvious to current and potential clients and customers that you work by appointment only. If you have your business hours listed as 8 am - 5pm, you should be there with the doors unlocked, lights on, and open to the public, unless you have a member's access-only business. Failing to adhere to business hours you have set, will rapidly ruin your reputation as a legitimate and professional business. Depending on the type of business you are running, sometimes you need to be there early. For example, if your business requires you to see a scheduled client, you should arrive at least 15 minutes early. If there is any preparation you need to do prior to seeing the client, such as making copies, finding their chart or file, or staging, you should arrive 15-30 minutes prior to your appointment.

If your business requires you to carry out any type of retail or formal business transaction at the open of business, under these circumstances, you should arrive early as well. If your business is one in which your main task at open is to make sure it is unlocked and open to the public, it may not be as important to arrive early, but you should be there on time. If your customers are under the impression that you open at 8 am and the doors are still locked at 8 am, that is problematic. I find it necessary to remind you of this, due to my personal experience. I once had a member who wanted out of their contract, and one of their excuses was that we didn't open on time. I was deeply hurt by this, because I knew this was not true however, I was guilty of arriving at the time we were supposed to be open, rather than early. Since our facility was a fitness center and all I had to do was show up and unlock the doors, I didn't think it was necessary to arrive any earlier than the time we were supposed to open.

When someone is looking for something they can use against you, they will find it and use it, especially if it is available to them. Be intentional about making daily decisions to prevent the possibility of offering such opportunities to those who wish to harm you, avoid compensation, or ruin your professional reputation. Showing up early reduces the risk of giving them that option. Many businesses would not agree with this, but I happen to be okay with releasing some individuals from contract prematurely. In my experience as a small business owner, clients or members that bring negativity, toxicity, and chaos to your business, aren't the kind of people you want as clients or members. Letting them go may be beneficial to both parties. You will get more members to cover that loss if you are running a professional company and are committed to excellence. One or two negative, bitter, or angry customers, members, or clients can have a negative impact on your public and professional reputation and to the morale and mood of your existing clients and members. Sometimes it is best to let them go whether they are locked into a contract or not. I am not suggesting you habitually release clients from contracts prematurely, after they have been initiated. I am simply suggesting that you consider the possibility that there will be some people you will not want in your establishment, due to their behavior, habits, disrespect, chaos, toxicity, and inability to follow the policies and procedures you have established.

> *Sometimes releasing toxic and unhealthy people in order to maintain peace in your business and in your life, is worth more than any amount of money.*

Focus on your clients who want to be in your establishment, respect and adhere to your policies and procedures, and see the value of the services and products being offered to them.

STOP GIVING YOUR SERVICES AND PRODUCTS
AWAY FOR FREE

I am a very giving person, so naturally I am a giving person also in business. After opening our fitness center, I found myself giving away free meal replacement shakes or giving discounts that were so low, we made no profit off of them. We were selling training packages for 50% less than the other area centers were selling the same or less training for, and we were allowing a few people to train for free for various reasons. To some extent we believed we had to be the Dollar store of fitness, because we were new and smaller than the big box gyms. Two things occurred that made me realize we had to stop giving away our products and services for free.

The first realization came after I noticed the people down the street who were also small and new, were charging nearly twice as much as we were, and their parking lot was always full. This proved that extreme discounts weren't the secret formula for success." It was more attributable to marketing strategy, and that they believed in their products and services. They knew what they were worth!

> *If you don't believe what your business offers*
> *is valuable, other people won't either.*

Providing quality services, products, and programs is crucial to building a successful business, however none of that means anything, if you don't believe it is of quality. As a Fashion Designer, you can start building a clothing line, and decide if your goal is to have your products sold in Wal-Mart, small boutiques, Neiman Marcus stores around the world, or only in your small personal boutique. The actual quality is a major factor in whether your garments end up in either store, however if you have Neiman Marcus quality, but a local corner store mindset, that is exactly where your clothing line will end up. Local corner stores are just as important and as necessary as larger corporations however, you have to decide your intended purpose and destination for your products and services and adopt that mindset. If you fail to do this, the destination and value of your products will be chosen for you. Starting out by selling your products in your own small personal boutique or corner store is great however, your overall long-term goal should be much bigger than that. I have purchased a few shirts, tights, and other fitness gear from discount retail stores, but no matter the quality, I typically assume it isn't high quality, otherwise it wouldn't be sold in a discount store. Unfortunately, this may not be true in many instances. This is what consumers assume when shopping for any item or service they are in need of.

There have been cases in which there was an item for sale in a high-end store that wasn't any better quality than items purchased in a discount store. For example, one year my husband and children purchased a designer purse as a gift for my Birthday. I thought WOW, I have a _____ purse! I won't mention the name, because it is not relevant. But after about five months, the straps were unraveling, and the purse was falling apart. I ended up throwing it away less than a year later. On the other hand, I'd had what most would call "no name" handbags that I'd used for years and they were still in pretty good shape. Don't be afraid that you will market your brand as a Neiman Marcus or Saks Fifth Avenue product, and it will come unraveled shortly after the purchase of your products or services. If you do the work, research, hire help, don't cut corners, and take your time, your products and services will become and remain of good quality. If for some reason there is some deterioration or unraveling in your products or services, don't give up right away. Do some troubleshooting to figure out what went wrong, fix it, test it, and try again. Most successful business owners have experienced some "unraveling" at some point, as I did with my first book. I had to go back to the drawing board more than once to repair the product. If you choose to go from Saks to small community "corner store" after the unraveling, due to lack of confidence in what you are offering, or because you ran into a few kinks in your product, you are making a huge mistake. You have to work out the kinks, perfect your product, and keep chopping at it until you get it just right. Many of the wealthiest moguls and business owners have had entire businesses fail and close, have filed bankruptcy more than once, as they were dumping loads of money into their businesses trying to make it work and refused to quit. Many of them have experienced severe and overwhelming stress as a result of trying to stop or prevent the unraveling or failure of a business they invested all of their time, energy, and resources into.

There are many people out there who might try to make you believe it is easy to start or maintain a business. They may try to make you think that you aren't supposed to make mistakes, or if you do make them, you simply aren't ready. If you hear that, it is usually coming from someone who hasn't done anything that great and hasn't taken very many risks. It's easy to notice and call out someone else's mistakes, while safely sitting on the bench. As long as you are in the game, you are taking risks and increasing your likelihood of success. If you are sitting on the bench you have no business criticizing those in the game. Get your pompoms out and cheer for them. One day you might be in the game and find yourself missing a few shots. At that point you will realize how much more challenging being in the game is, compared to sitting on the bench with a clean uniform, and free of sweat.

> *Most of the people who are at the top,*
> *have suffered significant losses and failures*
> *over the course of their career.*

In fact, if you do your research, you will find that many of them failed more times than they succeeded. They decided their product or service was of value, even when someone tried to tell them otherwise. They KNEW what they had to offer, and how much work and time they put into it, regardless of what others who hadn't witnessed their journey said. They were sure there was an audience, client, and consumer base for their product or services and they simply had to find that audience and deliver their products and services.

The other reason I decided I needed to stop giving away free products and services I'd poured so much of myself into, was that I realized the clients would just go find and pay someone else. For example, if someone is coming to our facility for free, they weren't committed to our facility. This left them open to purchase the same services somewhere else. There were individuals whom we allowed to train at our facility for free for various reasons. I would see those same people on social media posting videos of their workout at another facility, where they were paying for same services. We were allowing them to use our facility for free and they never mentioned us, rarely promoted us, and contributed very little to the well-being and growth of our business. To make matters even worse, they posted videos, gave raving reviews, and mention of how great the facilities and services were at the center they had to pay for. Since they had no financial obligation to us, their funds and loyalty were available to use elsewhere. Most of the members that are paying for programs or memberships at our facility are happy to promote it.

They appreciate our facility and attend regularly, because they are invested and value the programming and customer service. They are already invested, therefore they want to work-out where they are spending their money. Of course, there are exceptions to the rule, because we have many members or enrollees who maintain memberships at various facilities. In conclusion, I would like to reiterate that if you don't require your customers to pay for your services, they will pay for someone else's and use your free services as a backup, when they need a quick fix.

> *People are more likely to remain committed*
> *if they are financially invested.*

X.

CHAPTER X.

FINANCIAL STORMS

MONETARY DISTRESS

I experienced some financial challenges after starting a business. As previously mentioned, prior to becoming a business owner in my mid 30's, I had a decent paying state job, great benefits, and a pretty promising retirement plan. That sounded great and I wanted that, but I knew the job was not connected to my purpose. As a result, I could never be happy continuing there long-term. I had a Master's degree, great credit, a clinical license, and 17 years of professional experience. I thought I had paid my dues, had more than enough experience, and had the resources and credit to start my own business. I had dreamed of being a business owner for years and it was finally time to pursue that goal.

On several occasions, I tried to talk myself out of leaving my job, because it was very risky and somewhat irrational for several reasons. Each time I tried talking myself out of it, I would have some epiphany, revelatory moment, or some extraordinary confirmation. Something would happen on the job that would clearly confirm that there was no way I could remain there for another 25 years. I knew that the job was a blessing and a dream job for some, but it wasn't my blessing or dream. Eventually my husband and I decided that I would resign and get our first business started. I initiated the process decided on a name for our business, applied for our LLC, and initiated a business line of credit.

Once we opened our business, we knew the extent of the initial investment we'd made. We had never invested anything close to the amount of money we did in *Club Exhilaration* on anything. We remained diligent about spending wisely. We didn't shop very much, we stopped taking vacations, and we changed our overall lifestyle. We refrained from making unnecessary purchases as we knew that we had new financial obligations that also required financial sacrifices.

It is important to assess your revenue and expenses regularly to ensure you are increasing your profit. This is especially important when running a brick and mortar business since you will likely incur more overhead and expenses.

> *There is a significant difference between running a brick and mortar business or a virtual business.*

The expenses are far more extensive due to overhead, contracts, permits, repairs, equipment, payroll, and so on. Fortunately, I can tell you what I experienced, not just what I have read or heard.

Business ownership isn't all fun, easy, or good times. There are more fun days than not, you breeze through some months in the black, but there are sometimes months in the red, where your expenses exceed your revenue. Many business owners fail to tell you about this aspect of business ownership.

We remembered that we had been faithful tithers for seven years prior to opening our first business, which was one of the reasons we were able to open the business in the first place, among other financial endeavors and investments. My husband and I had a discussion and agreed that our faith, consistent and faithful tithing and hard work, was what got us to the point where we had the confidence and resources to open a business. Therefore it was exactly that principle which would keep us there. We resumed tithing and within a short period of time we started to feel relief in our financial status. In addition, we decided we had to start putting more money into savings whether we had bills or not. It didn't matter if we made $8,000 or $25,000 in a month, we were spending most of it on bills. We simply weren't paying ourselves. We decided we weren't going to satisfy the financial obligations from our initial investment overnight, and that it would be more of a marathon than a sprint. As a result we decided to pace ourselves and pay ourselves in the process.

> *You must pay yourself prior to paying everyone else.*
> *Otherwise, you are working for everyone else.*

The best way to pay yourself is to contribute to savings regularly. Having more income than ever and seeing all of it spent on bills can be quite discouraging. It makes a lot of business owners throw in the towel prematurely, because they feel they are working harder than ever, with no return or financial gain. You should also evaluate your finances regularly to make sure there aren't any other necessary changes to address.

> *An approach or strategy that worked*
> *for you financially in the first year does not guarantee*
> *it will work for you in the third year.*

Figure out what is working, what is not working, and possible strategies you have not yet tried. My husband and business partner and I continue to meet regularly to discuss our financial affairs and revise our financial plans as needed. Just like anything else, our financial plans should be constantly re-evaluated and revised.

GETTING THROUGH THE FINANCIAL CHALLENGES OF BUSINESS OWNERSHIP

Find ways to earn additional income by sharing your expertise with others locally and globally, if possible. There is very little investment required in sharing your expertise in a book, outside of editing, marketing, and publishing. Sharing your expertise through speaking engagements also requires very little expense. Your speaking engagements can be connected to your book, business, or both. You can also speak about other topics you are experienced in, or as requested by the host. When pursuing additional or supplemental income, be careful about accruing additional or unnecessary expenses. Hire staff a little at a time and add as your revenue increases. Payroll is usually your biggest expense once your business starts to grow, so be progressive and smart when hiring.

Below are a few suggested tips on preventing or getting through financial distress as a business owner.

1. During months in which you are in the black and have a surplus in funds, **try to pay off expenses.** Pay ahead of time since you don't know what the next months will bring, and having a credit on your electricity bill might be beneficial. Don't spend your extra earnings just because you have it. Remember you may have to temporarily sacrifice some of your shopping and vacations until your business is thriving, financially stable and

self-sustaining. For a few years your shopping will consist of purchasing supplies, equipment, and utilities for your new business and expenses at home. For a short period of time, your vacation will be a staycation at your new business.

2. **Get help with marketing and advertising**. Keep in mind that in most cases you have to spend money to make money.

3. **Be creative with cost saving initiatives with your staff.** Implement procedures in your place of business in order to save money. In our business there are usually a few hours in the middle of the day where hardly anyone comes in. We started turning the lights out during that time. I wonder how much money we could have saved had we thought of that during the first year.

4. **Compare prices for supplies.** Waiting until you are out of supplies forces you to buy on an impulse and in a hurry, because you need them right away. If you order or purchase supplies ahead of time you can save money by comparing prices.

5. **Save all of your receipts and invoices.** At the end of the year you will need them for taxes. If your expenses exceeded your revenue for that year, you certainly want to be able to prove that with proper documentation at tax time. This will benefit you significantly as it will reduce the amount of taxes you owe and possibly result in a refund due to a well-documented loss. It would be a shame if a financial loss occurred in your business and you weren't able to prove it. I would opt for not having a loss in business, however the harsh truth is that in the beginning, it is likely this will be the case for most small businesses. If so, you want to be able to provide proper documentation when it's time to file taxes.

6. **Consult with a professional financial advisor.** They might be able to help you develop a more effective strategy in saving, managing, and investing money.

7. Don't lose it! **Hang in there** and realize financial challenges come with the territory. You must have endurance if you want to see your business succeed. If it were easy, everyone would be doing it. This is why so many people want to open a business, but choose not to. It is a challenge, can be exhausting, and you must have what some call "sticktoitivity," which is the ability to stick to what you started.

8. **Be creative,** don't get complacent, and keep things interesting for your clients. In some businesses you will lose and gain customers often, but make sure it isn't because you are failing to make them feel appreciated, you aren't providing quality services or products, or you have gotten lazy.

9. **Save money** no matter what and don't put all of your eggs in one basket. What I mean by this is; open a couple of different accounts. I recommend having accounts at more than one bank. This will allow you to save, and allocate funds for different expenses. If you are having trouble saving because expenses are due as soon as you receive funds in your account, you will end up with no money to spend for yourself. I recommend setting a specific amount you are going to save each week and putting it in an account that you don't have a debit card or checkbook for. This will prevent spending it when you need extra cash, because it will be more difficult to get to the money. I typically tell people $50-$100 a week is a great starting point with saving. You have to start somewhere. You can always increase your weekly contribution when possible. Your goal should be to increase that weekly contribution. No matter the financial bind you might find

yourself in, don't spend money from that pot! If you face your worst financial nightmare, this pot of money should remain off limits and not be accessed. The reason for this is because as a business owner, especially during the first five to seven years, you might have more expenses than income. There is a deep hole that you are digging yourself out of from your initial investment for years. You will continue to see growth in income, however it is unlikely that number will exceed your expenses for a while, depending on the type of business you own. This isn't the case for all. This is mainly for those who start a business that requires a substantial initial investment prior to building a client base or earning revenue. Some examples of such investments are; acquiring a building, exterior signage, construction or renovations, hiring staff, equipment, software, computers and technological equipment. This wouldn't apply to most web based business or home based businesses. If you spend every dollar you receive on bills you will always be broke, you will be depressed, live in agony, and will begin to resent the very thing you had passion for. You will possibly question why you started in the first place, you will experience ongoing anxiety over financial trouble, and you will be setting yourself up for failure. When in a financial bind, if you can't borrow from a loved one and have no choice but to borrow from yourself, don't forget to pay the loan off with interest. Give yourself a timeline to pay your loan with yourself off, just as you would with anyone else. Be sure to pay your loved ones off in a timely fashion when they loan you money, so that they know they can trust you. You never know when you might need them again.

10. **Schedule a consultation session with a professional** to help get your plan in place. This should be someone who will

help you with a business plan, blue print, strategic planning, and refer you to other necessary professionals.

> *As it relates to business,*
> *I find it extremely important to mention,*
> ## IT IS OKAY TO BOW OUT.

As I specified previously, the sacrifices you will make to run a business are much more than you could ever imagine until you are knee deep into business ownership. There is a big difference between reading about business ownership, watching someone else do it, and actually owning and running one yourself. Some sacrifices are so extreme and painful that they are quite difficult to bounce back from. For example, some of the business owners I have spoken or become familiar with, report circumstances such as an onset of health problems, weight gain, burnout, compassion fatigue, unhealthy or nonexistent social life, failed relationships, and believe it or not, reproductive issues. All of this can be due to stressful conditions.

There may come a time in business ownership in which you have to throw in the towel. Many successful business owners have experienced several failed businesses prior to having a successful one. Some business owners have closed businesses and started a completely different business due to an increased need for the other business in their area. They discovered that their expertise and experience is stronger in the area that is in demand, or they weren't seeing the desired financial return on their previous business. You don't have to do what you've always done, it's okay to change things up. Starting something new outside of your initial start-up does not equate to failure. Sometimes this equates to success because you aren't beating a dead path. Don't feel as if you've failed if you have to close your business, pull your book from the shelves, or sell your company. This is more common than you would imagine.

Prior to making the final decision to close, you should first conduct an analysis of the risks and benefits involved with remaining open versus closing your doors. Next, determine if you are able to handle the risks involved with remaining open. Once you have arrived at a decision, wait for a few days and consult with your mentor or business consultant prior to taking action. Most importantly, pray about it. Typically, if you wait and listen, you will find that you either get some sort of confirmation that you are making the right decision, or an affirmation that you are exactly where you are supposed to be. Sometimes when things seem challenging or impossible you might find that your business is succeeding or showing progress in areas you haven't considered and remaining in business is less of a risk than you'd thought. This confirmation can come in many forms, so pay close attention. It may come by way of a very clear and accurate spreadsheet that indicates a critical financial need for closure, or significant financial gain, a letter or visit from a federal, state or local entity, or something of a spiritual nature.

There was a time that we considered closing our business due to slow or insufficient revenue, lack of sleep, frustration, and because family vacations had become nonexistent. One morning, my husband and I discussed the benefits of closing, and determined we'd had enough. We were tired of working 60 - 70 hours a week, sleeping four to six hours a night, and having no family or vacation time. After that discussion, we were leaning towards throwing in the towel. We held hands in our office and prayed together, prior to his leaving to go to his other job. Less than an hour after he left our business to go to work, we had a member come in to work out. This was our very first member that checked in that day. As soon as she walked in, her first words were, "I love coming here! It feels so good to be in here! You guys have no idea how many people you are helping with this place. I bet everyone else feels as good as I feel every time I walk in the door. I am so glad I heard about this place."

I immediately sent my husband a text message stating,

"He said no. It isn't time."

My husband replied with, "He as in HE??"

Of course, I responded with, "Yes, HE!"

We both chuckled, took that as our creator saying hang in there, you are doing a great job, and you are where you are supposed to be. That was the end of that conversation. At that point, we knew we had to stay in it, and so we did. We listened to the instructions we received from our creator and remained obedient. God started to turn things around for us as we kept working hard to live out the purpose he assigned to us. We started to see promotions, collaborations and partnerships, and more community engagements.

> *Just as it will be apparent when it is time to pull the plug, it will be clear when you must sit still and finish the race.*

CHAPTER XI.

PROTECTING YOUR BRAND

During the first few years of business ownership you might experience financial hardship. Due to this financial hardship you might become vulnerable to giving in to or accepting invitations to collaborate with or work for other entities in order to make up for financial loss or help make ends meet. The two most important points I would like to make here are: supplementing your income is a great idea when you are self-employed, however, be careful about how you pursue it

Once you have made the decision to work for yourself, open a business, or become an entrepreneur, you should consider ways in which you can bring in extra revenue while you are in the start-up or building phase. For some businesses this timeframe is anywhere from a few months to a few years. For other businesses this building phase could last well over five years, depending on the nature of the business, the demand for products and services offered, marketing strategies, and overall management of the business.

> *As a business owner you should have*
> *more than one stream of income.*

Most business owners have found that writing books, hosting seminars, booking speaking engagements, and securing contractual agreements with other companies are the best options in creating new streams or sources of revenue. These options allow you to maintain a flexible schedule so that you are available for growth and future projects while promoting diversity and creativity in your experience as a business owner.

During this time, it is very easy to find yourself under the umbrella of another business or entity due to opportunities. But please beware, because getting into a situation where you are offered money or services for your partnership isn't always as free as it sounds. Remember that you and what you are offering is valuable, and you can't compromise your brand for free services, a paycheck, office space, publicity, or connections.

> *There will be individuals who will recognize*
> *your great value, need something you have*
> *to help them get what they want,*
> *and will try using you for their benefit*
> *rather than yours.*

One of the major concerns with working for another company or being housed under their umbrella, is that when someone pursues you based on what you can give or do for them, they abandon you once they get it. If they didn't have a prosperous business, they wanted to tap into a different demographic that they believe you have captured. Or perhaps they want to further develop another facet of their business and use your unique abilities to help them get there.

Once they achieve their goal, it is possible you will become disposable to them, depending on the nature of your relationship.

In addition, beware of individuals wanting to "piggy back" on your business. I am a firm believer in collaborations and partnerships, however there are people out there who seek success and others who can help them achieve it, while not bringing much to the table. There will be individuals or companies that may offer you money or services in order to utilize your space, while taking notes on everything you do, adopting your business practices, and learning everything about your original approach. They will then find the person or entity that can take them to the next level, while leaving your facility or office space worn down and deteriorated. They will refuse to offer repairs or upgrades on any of your equipment or space and simply move on. Once again, they have no more use or need for you since they got everything they wanted. Rather than trying to grow with you, or help you grow beyond where you are now, they will do that somewhere else with the next individual or company they believe can help them with the next step. This is not wrong, nor should they feel obligated to remain in collaboration with you once they are ready to move on. However, you should be aware of this possibility before moving forward and deciding whom you allow in and the fees, contracts, and expectations that you will put in writing.

> *You should always have a written and signed contract that spells out the rules, boundaries, expectations, and fees, with anyone you hire or do business with.*

95

These are very important factors that help protect your brand. When partnering with another individual or entity, be sure not to allow them to get you into a position, where it appears that you are working for them. You must set yourself apart at all costs. If you are renting a space in a place that offers different services or is not affiliated with your business, make sure that your marketing strategies are creative enough to communicate to your audience, that you are an independent business. It is also important to communicate this to customers and clients during initial meetings. Once you are under the roof or umbrella of another company or entity, it is easy to become one of their employees and forget about your vision for your own company. You have to determine if earning or saving a few extra dollars is really necessary and worth taking time away from your purpose and vision.

> *There are cases in which a new business owner*
> *will have to take on a secondary job*
> *or remain in current one, until they are earning*
> *a sufficient profit from their own business.*

I am simply suggesting that you are careful about the type of business you get involved with. For example, it probably isn't a good idea to associate yourself with a company that is trying to build their brand at this time. It doesn't make much sense to build someone else's brand while you are still trying to build yours, unless they are substantially contributing to building your brand as well. This is one of the reasons partnerships are important. Depending on the contract, most partnerships permit each individual party to remain independent outside of the collaborative agreement.

People who don't want to see you succeed beyond their success or who are more interested in what you can offer them or their brand, will try very hard to use you to promote, represent, and build their brand. As a business owner you don't hire or collaborate with someone who will not somehow move your business forward, so keep that in mind. When I hire an individual to work in our facility, I expect them to be loyal to our brand, promote the business, and alert us regarding positions elsewhere. We ensure there aren't any conflicts of interest and that their new or outside employment will not interfere or impede with their ability to adequately represent our company. Obviously, I would like for each employee to benefit from working for us as much as we would benefit from them being a part of our company. I try to keep in mind that other business owners think in this manner as well. Therefore, when they are trying to recruit me, it is for the growth of their company rather than mine, or just as much as mine. If both parties benefit somewhat equally, the likelihood that their arrangement will be productive and healthy is high.

Many business owners have to temporarily utilize office space from others in order to save money.

> *When possible, it is important to secure your own work space.*

It doesn't have to be fancy, large, or elaborate. Be sure to maintain your own logo, email, website, and brochures. If you make the decision to partner with another person or business, remaining separate entities is difficult if you are using the same letterhead, website, and literature. If your goal is to communicate that you are one in the same with your business partner using the same website, brochures, and logo, is perfectly fine.

Having your own space leaves less room for confusion or questions about who you are, what you offer, and whether you are affiliated with someone else. It can also protect business relationships that are important to you. For example, you might have a great business partner, the two of you work very well together, but you notice that each of you has some personality flaws or traits that might become problematic, if you worked in the same space every day. In such a case, you should think really hard before agreeing to share an office.

You can't collaborate with everyone. There are some people in your industry that are great at what they do, however their personal life might not line up with your professional reputation. For example, as a married woman, a mother, licensed therapist, and a business owner, I take my personal and professional reputation very seriously. If I were to enter a business partnership with someone who has different morals and values than I do, it could be an unhealthy partnership. I like to use the biblical concept of being unequally yoked. Being in a business partnership with someone who has different morals, values, boundaries, and ethics, can be very similar to being married to someone with such different principles. It could become disastrous and costly.

> *Social media can be very dangerous and a major threat to one's personal and professional reputation.*

If you are a professional or a business owner and you are posting pictures of yourself partying every weekend, constantly venting about people you are upset with while using profanity, sharing personal relationship problems, and other inappropriate and unprofessional behavior, you should stop immediately, especially if you want to protect your brand. If you have been engaging in such behavior, the damage has already been done, and you have probably painted an undesirable picture of yourself to others. Don't become angry or surprised if you find that others don't want to partner with you or invest in your business.

Acquiring a client base and support from your community is challenging enough without posting damaging photos and videos on social media. Be careful about opening a business with someone who publicly or privately carries on or portrays themselves in an unprofessional manner. It doesn't mean either party has to have a squeaky clean reputation. Just make sure you get involved with professionals and entities that have worked as hard at protecting their personal and professional reputation, as you have. Although I have personal and professional friends and partners from all walks of life, I tend to refrain from connecting with people professionally who haven't worked as hard at protecting their reputation. Do not allow your business to fail as a result of someone else's negligence, lack of self-control, or professionalism. Reputation isn't everything, but when you are building a brand, you can't afford to risk your audience not connecting with you or not trusting you, because you lack self-control on social media, post provocative, vulgar and promiscuous pictures, out of control party habits, or any other personal details shouldn't be shared on social media.

> *It is important to remember that your reputation is a major part of your brand.*

Everything you do on the clock and off the clock matters and is giving your brand either life or death. You have potential customers, clients, and partners on your friend list, that are sitting back watching and judging everything you do and say. They want to believe they can trust you and that you truly are the professional you say you are. If you lack the self-control necessary to refrain from appearing unprofessional on social media, maybe you should disengage and instead hire a volunteer to manage your social media accounts for you.

I am pretty sure someone reading this book has no idea what is professional and what isn't. Referring to themselves as a professional or expert in any industry while maintaining an unprofessional profile on social media confirms that many people simply don't have a clue what professionalism looks like. Some believe they can post what they want on their social media pages, simply because they are an adult and it is their page. The truth is, the profile is referred to as a "public profile" because it is public. Nothing you post on social media, text messages, or the internet in general is private. Many people believe that if they aren't showing the world everything they have, as in the good, bad, and the ugly, they aren't being genuine. There is a time and place for everything, and some of the bad and ugly needs to stay out of the public eye and should only be shared with loved ones. I understand transparency and the need to be an open book however, when you are building a brand, revealing every aspect of your personal life may not be a good idea. Posting racist comments, strong political views, or judgmental religious views could be offensive to potential clients or partnerships. I know some of my readers will disagree and vow that their race, religious, and political views are their right and whomever disagrees or is offended, they would consider undesirable for their business anyway. This is absurd and self-sabotaging behavior for a business owner.

A person's personal beliefs should not matter, but in our society they certainly do matter. Act accordingly! Keep in mind that in today's world even CEO's, celebrities and people in the public eye are increasingly scrutinized and need to be watchful of their public statements as it can ruin their reputation, business and career. Consider this, it is wise that you always communicate in the utmost civilized, all-inclusive, just and nondiscriminatory manner. In fact, your social media platform is open to public, which makes your every post a public statement.

Most of us are pretty serious when it comes to our religious practices and beliefs. In fact, we might agree that as professionals and business owners we should keep our stance on race or opinions regarding race and politics out of our public profile, but how dare you suggest I tone down my religious stance? Many people have had bad experiences with church, feel they are constantly being judged by religious people, don't believe in God, or are simply turned off by discussion of religion. As believers in God, if you are always publicly condemning people who don't believe in the same principles as you do, making judgmental religious statements, or posting very heavy religious material on your social media pages and during speaking engagements, you will lose a lot of potential clients or customers.

Be encouraging, positive, and motivating
rather than condemning or judgmental
when you post comments related to religion.

This might draw people in rather than push them away. By the way, preaching to people is not always the best approach for encouraging others to develop a relationship with God. Often, their experience with you will be the determining factor as to whether they want to give it a try.

> *You were not hired to be the Global Pastor for social media, however your life should be the testimony, evidence, and preaching to peak other people's curiosity and desire to know more about God.*

When they come into your presence or place of business, they will know there is something different and special about you that sets you apart. If your target population is strictly people with the same religious beliefs as yours, then this principle does not apply to you.

Many of us become offended when people whom we thought would support us don't. There are many individuals that I have known for years, whom I have a good relationship with, have been to my house, and are connected to me in various ways, that choose to visit other professionals for services or help. Yes, this bothers me, but I can't force them to invest in services for physical or mental health from me. In addition, I can't become angry with everyone who does not have a membership to my health club or seeks counseling with another professional. I have given free memberships, counseling sessions, personal and group training sessions to people who went across town or down the street and paid twice as much somewhere else, as they would have paid with me. Some have attributed it to better hours, childcare offered, and other reasons. In most cases they didn't go to the other facility very often, therefore, didn't use their 24-hour access nor did they take their kids with them more than ten times out of the year. The idea of having "more" options with a larger company that they don't really use, was more important than investing in the same services with a smaller business, owned by someone they know personally. I had to accept that they wanted to pay twice as much money for a place that was already making millions of dollars a year, and didn't care whether they were there or not, rather than invest in and help build a smaller company in which the owners and employees cared about them, and their membership or purchasing of services was critical to the operation and survival of the smaller business.

You too will have to face this harsh reality when or if you decide to become a business owner. Keep in mind, not everyone will support you, simply because you aren't big enough, corporate enough, fit enough, smart enough, or you just simply aren't enough in their opinion. Some will not support you because you are too much in their eyes and they couldn't possibly stand the idea of being a part of you excelling beyond where you are and becoming more. You have to accept this is reality and move on.

> *Focus your energy on the people that do support you rather than the ones that don't.*

XII.

CHAPTER XII.

MAINTAINING ONCE YOU ARE OUT OF THE DARKNESS

Hopefully, once you are at least a couple of years into business ownership, you're finally seeing the light at the end of the tunnel. You've probably experienced the worst of your start up, and are in the process of repairing credit if necessary, paying off loans and debts, and returning to some sense of normalcy at work and at home. It is highly likely that you are now able to spend more quality time with family and resume vacation time. This is a good time to reflect on what you have lost along the way, what you have maintained or gained, the overall health of your family and business, personal mental and physical health, and how all of these things will impact your life moving forward. This is also a great time to engage in self-evaluation and refocusing.

Hopefully your losses were minimal however, if your personal or professional losses were excessive or extreme, if you have lost things like your home or other repossessions, or you have recently separated or divorced from your spouse, I encourage you to seek counseling from a licensed professional. Financial distress is one of the leading causes of divorce. Some relationships simply aren't strong enough to survive such stress.

> *Self-evaluation is critical once you have surpassed some of your initial business goals.*

Enrolling into Personal Counseling will allow you to sort through the wide range of emotions you might be experiencing as a result of such significant loss.

This is a time to begin journaling, if you have not already. Asking yourself questions such as:

What can I do to remain on track while moving forward?

What did I do or not do that contributed to initial problems with the start up?

What can I do to prevent some of those same problems from resurfacing?

What areas of my business remain underdeveloped?

What areas of business are thriving?

Do I need help?

How can I increase revenue while reducing costs?

What are my business goals for the next 3 months, 6 months, and year?

At this point you need to focus on short-term rather than long-term goals. You still have a lot of growth that needs to occur in a short period of time in order to remain in business and not become one of the statistics. This is not a good time to become lazy, comfortable, complacent, or lose focus. This is where you really want to hone in on where you are going next and what is going to set your business apart from others. After answering the aforementioned questions, it is a good idea to set up a strategic planning meeting with your business coach. If you do not have a business coach or mentor and can't afford one, seek out a local business owner and ask for mentoring.

More than likely you have learned and grown quite a bit over the first couple of years of running your business. There are numerous reasons your circle gets smaller as you progress. One of the most common-ones is that everyone will not grow as you do. People who aren't committed to growth and change and who don't have the amount of responsibility that you do, will sometimes accuse you of treating them differently or not making enough time for them. They might be completely inconsiderate of the fact that you have been working hard for the past couple of years while trying to maintain your business and keep your family intact, which means you have not had much time for a social life. The most ridiculous given reason for losing a few friends along the way, is because according to them, YOU'VE CHANGED! My thoughts are, if you have not changed you are not ready for the next phase of business ownership. Change often indicates growth.

> *Your true friends will give you the space, support, and understanding required to accomplish your goals.*

They will also welcome the changes you make in your work ethic, commitment to excellence, ability to prioritize things and people in your life, and your determination to seeing through what you've started.

Unfortunately, you might also lose some family members for some of the same reasons along the way. It will hurt when you have to walk away from people who were once important to you, or when they choose to walk away from you. But, you will recover. Once you have succeeded, be sure to thank those who supported you, believed in you, and celebrated you from start to finish. The people that remain with you at the celebrating stage deserve to celebrate with you.

The attendance at the celebratory table might look quite different than what you had hoped for or anticipated. The people sitting with you didn't take your journey personally, they didn't become offended or angry when you chose to not satisfy their personal needs and wants at a time when it would have cost you everything. They chose to love and support you without judgment along the way. Most importantly, they believed in you and encouraged you to believe in yourself.

Self-care is critical because you have been working and sacrificing harder than you ever have. It is now time to take some time off, plan a vacation, take pleasure in some of your money for the first time since you opened, and enjoy your family. You have certainly earned this vacation. We waited three years before we took our first vacation. Because we waited, we were able to have a stress-free vacation knowing our bills were paid, our staff were paid, the facility was running properly, and everything would be just fine in our absence.

This is also a good time to consider shortening your hours if you have been working sunrise to sunset. This might require hiring help to cover the additional hours, depending on the nature of your business.

In order to ensure you will maintain good health throughout your years of business ownership, this is a great time to evaluate whether you are taking care of your physical health. If you have gotten away from living a healthy lifestyle, or you never have tried to live a healthy lifestyle in the past, this is a great time to start. Taking care of yourself and doing things to promote good health will increase the likelihood of your being around to enjoy your years of business ownership and a happy retirement. Living a healthy lifestyle starts with simple things such as adopting a heart healthy diet, remaining hydrated, getting seven to nine hours of sleep each night, keeping your stress level down, and engaging in daily exercise. For additional information on living a healthy lifestyle, you are welcome to purchase my book titled: *Nurture your Body - Overcoming and Preventing Obesity*. It is available on my website and all online bookstores, including Amazon and Barnes and Noble.

At this point you might have to schedule weekly family time and one on one time with your spouse. It is highly likely that during the long work hours, you have become somewhat distant from the people you love the most.

> *Scheduling a weekly family night, game night, or some type of activity, is a great idea.*

Family time does not have to be elaborate, exhausting, or expensive. Children enjoy simple moments such as everyone being home at the same time, which allows us to sit down and enjoy a family meal or watch a movie together. Just being connected with each other and actually present on a regular basis is important. When quality family time is limited, requesting that everyone "power off" their devices during time spent together is a good idea. No one's business, education, or social life will fall apart because they weren't available for an hour, once or twice each week. Consider having everyone turn their devices off for an hour or two.

XIII.

CHAPTER XIII.

QUITTING IS NOT AN OPTION

We kept moving forward, we had goals, we had a plan, and we had faith. You can do the same with your business and with your family. Remember, growth is an ongoing process. You should always have intentions and plans to grow in every area of your life, at all times. For some people, growth means planning for retirement. For others, growth might mean you start providing services out of your home, or on a travel or onsite basis and work your way up to eventually occupying your own office or building. You might start out as a one-man or one-woman show, but work your way up to having staff in place to make things run more efficiently and professionally. Having a solid strategic plan, revising the plan when necessary, recruiting help when needed, securing the right resources to execute and carry out the plan, and knowing when your plan isn't working, are all critical to your success.

There will be times when you feel like you are failing, you are exhausted, and you want to quit.

A major component of being a successful
and effective business owner
is overcoming challenges and obstacles.

If you aren't resilient or lack endurance, you might want to consider staying in the safe zone of your 9-5 career. Remaining in your 9-5 career is certainly not a bad thing, nor is it a loss. In fact, you can run a lucrative business as a CEO, President, Vice President, Manager, or shift supervisor at a company that you didn't create and be just as or even more successful than if you were running your own. Whichever route you choose, decide to do it with excellence, confidence, and intention. Make the choice to never do anything halfway.

> *In order to be successful, you have to go all the way in and completely sell out to your ideas and your business.*

There will also be times in which things get stressful, chaotic, or outright unhealthy, at home or at work. Remembering why you launched your business and why you started a family is important when things get tough. Recapture the feelings and thoughts that you felt right before and right after you opened the doors of your business for the first time, and how you felt in the delivery room giving birth to your first child. When things get rough in your marriage as you are going through this journey to greatness, pull out your wedding pictures and reconnect with the joy you felt that day. Revisiting the beginning and the "why" will help you refocus and put things back into perspective. Hopefully you will reignite the fire that you once had for the things you desired and were most passionate about, the things that exhaustion and fatigue have clouded over time.

Fighting for your dreams should be a priority. Two things to keep in mind are, your dreams shouldn't be your only priority, and your family should always be your first priority and a major part of your dream. If you have big dreams that don't include your family, remaining connected to them will become increasingly difficult throughout your journey. Some people are at a high risk for losing their family and all that is important to them just to achieve their dreams. Many people may claim that everything they do is for the sake of their family, but that doesn't always prove to be true. If this is your notion, please stop and ask yourself the following questions:

Is this what my family wants or is this what I want for my family?

Do I have the same goals and dreams as my family?

Is this going to make me happy or will my entire family be happy once I have achieved this?

Is this bringing my family together or further apart?

In many cases things become so stressful and difficult that at some point we forget the things that are causing the most stress in our lives are actually the things that we wanted the most. Remember that this was YOUR dream and you can't stop dreaming about it or fighting for it just because it isn't easy. If it were easy everyone would have a business, lead sales position, a supervisory or management role at work, or have been promoted to a top executive job. If it were easy everyone would have a great marriage with happy, healthy, and thriving kids, a nice home, and frequent family vacations. If it were easy very few people would get divorced, close their business, or lose their job.

> *Everything that we dream of or once dreamed of,*
> *will be the most difficult to achieve*
> *and the very things we have to fight the hardest for.*

Opening a business, maintaining a business, raising children, taking care of yourself mentally and physically, and remaining happily married in the process of doing all of the above is in some ways similar to a triathlon. You can't be just a runner. You have to run, swim, and bike for more miles than you ever imagined you could.

> *If you have the endurance of a sprinter*
> *and sign up for a triathlon, you are definitely in trouble*
> *and are setting yourself up for failure.*

You have to train for the right event. Athletes who participate in triathlons train long and hard for months to improve endurance, reduce the risk of injury, and finish strong. If you have been conditioning to run a 5k (3.1 miles) and on race day you get on the course for an Ironman triathlon, you might barely make it through the 2.4 mile swim if at all, but you certainly won't make it through the 112 mile bike ride, and the 26.2 mile marathon run. In most cases the participant will either not complete the event or complete the event with severe injuries. In some cases, training for the wrong event will result in injury and failure to complete the race.

Finally, in some cases the participant will not only sustain injuries and not complete the race, but will most likely never compete again. Some will never compete again because the injuries sustained are so serious, that they physically won't be able to compete. In some cases, mental injuries are too severe, such as the level of fear, shame, and embarrassment from the intense moment of inadequacy and failure. These consequences will hinder them from regaining their confidence to try again. As a result, that particular participant will never use their God given gift to walk in their purpose due to lack of endurance, failure to plan for the event, and crippling fear as a result of their inability to bounce back after failure.

XIV.

CHAPTER XIV.

ENDURANCE IS CRITICAL

You might ask, how does one "train" for endurance in business and family? The best way to start is to read. Reading is information, therefore training. This will allow you to get ideas from others who have already done what you are trying to accomplish, without reinventing the wheel. In addition, reading allows you to gain information and perspective from various people with different backgrounds and experiences. Studying books on business ownership can be similar to getting coaching from various experienced professionals, if you choose the right authors and material. There are also numerous books available on business practices, business ownership, and all things related to business. In addition, there are thousands of books on the market on family issues, interpersonal relationships, child rearing, maintaining a healthy marriage, communication, and more.

ENDURANCE TRAINING FOR
ASPIRING BUSINESS OWNERS

Do your homework. You need to develop a blueprint or framework from which you will build upon early in the process. This blueprint should include a mission for your business, a vision statement, an identified target population, and selected services or products you will provide. Research the competition and the market in your area, perform a cost analysis, and start working on a business plan. There are numerous companies that specialize in providing assistance in developing business strategy.

When analyzing the costs associated with opening your business, make sure you remember to include things like insurance, certifications, equipment, staff, supplies, annual inspections, fees for professional associations you belong to, trainings and conferences. There is much more to opening and running a business than paying rent and utilities. Our start-up costs for our fitness center exceeded start-up costs for my counseling practice by far, due to the sophisticated and expensive equipment required for a gym. All I needed for my counseling practice was office furniture, computer, basic supplies, and monthly rent and utilities. In addition, I have professional development fees and memberships which require annual dues, my website, billing service, and internet ads.

> *I find it necessary to reiterate the importance of connecting with a business mentor.*

This could make the difference between working harder and working smarter. Typically, business coaches are pretty costly, but hiring one can make the difference between running an organized and successful business with reduced risk for legal trouble, or running a failing business with inadequate business practices, policies, and procedures. If you find that hiring a business coach or mentor simply isn't in your budget, try finding a successful small local business owner that you admire and ask them to commit to coaching you for a reasonable fee.

Another necessary approach to becoming a successful business owner is connecting with other aspiring or existing business owners for networking and sharing information. There are various networking groups for small business owners and entrepreneurs. The best places to find such groups are through your local Chamber of Commerce, and local BNI groups. There are also app's that offer such networking opportunities. I personally like the "Meetup" app. There are various groups you can join, based on personal and professional interests. Most groups have monthly meetings, at which time they share information, provide training, and network.

> *Spending time around other business owners or*
> *aspiring business entrepreneurs, can provide you*
> *with general information that you would*
> *ordinarily have to research or pay for,*
> *as well as opportunities for networking.*

Eventually you will need to secure a physical location for your business, unless you have opted to operate exclusively online. Shop around and avoid committing to the first thing offered. You will find that many commercial property owners go strictly by the book on dollar amount per square foot of space. In some cases, commercial property owners or managers are more flexible and willing to negotiate monthly rent based on various factors and circumstances. For example, if the property space has been vacant for a long period of time, is in a hidden location and doesn't offer adequate visibility, might be in need of repairs, or numerous other reasons. Don't be afraid to negotiate the terms of your lease.

Passing city and fire inspections can be quite stressful. Many of the older buildings don't pass inspections the first time, due to outdated plumbing or electrical wiring. These are all issues the landlord or property owner should address. Contact your city government buildings and inspections department to apply for a commercial occupancy permit. They will then set up an appointment for your inspections. You will not be issued an occupancy permit until you have passed all required inspections by the city and then your local Fire Chief. Once you pass inspections, the city will issue an occupancy permit. The city inspections are only conducted prior to opening a business, but fire inspections will occur annually. You will be required to pay an annual fee for the fire inspections. If you are running a business without having passed the city and fire inspections and an occupancy permit, you are more than likely operating illegally. In some cases, you will be required to have a license in addition to your occupancy permit. This depends on the type of business you have. For example, an establishment that sells or serves alcohol must have a license to do so, and an establishment that serves food or beverages of any sort is required to have a food service certification from their local health department. Check with your local city buildings and inspections department to confirm the process for commercial occupancy in your area and what is required for the type of business you are opening.

Changing your way of thinking is also critical for survival and completion of the journey and assignment.

> *Your thoughts are very powerful and can set the course for your entire life.*

In fact, this is the most important component in endurance training. Most people resort to negative thoughts once life becomes stressful, difficult, and unmanageable. Negative thinking under these circumstances can be self-defeating and debilitating.

Training your mind to see the good in every situation is instrumental for survival throughout the most difficult times of your life. While we were in the height of our struggle as new business owners and were experiencing financial challenges, we focused on how much fun we were having, how many people we were helping transform their bodies and improve their quality of life, and the reasons we decided to open our business in the first place. This helped us to remain in a positive and resilient mindset.

Having tried something and failing at it, makes you familiar with the subject matter. Having tried something and succeeding, makes you experienced in that area. Having tried something, failing, and eventually succeeding, makes you qualified in that area. Having succeeded, then failed after a period of success, and being able to bounce back from the devastation of the failure and succeed again, makes you an expert. Having never tried makes your opinion or input in this area irrelevant and your opinion holds very little weight, if any at all. When it comes to business, let's strive to be at minimum qualified prior to trying to help someone else in the area.

Being an expert will increase your chances of long-term success at helping others, so embrace, appreciate, and share both your victories and failures.

ENDURANCE TRAINING FOR FAMILY

One of the most basic approaches to being fit for the long haul in your marriage and as a parent, is surrounding yourself with other families. You see the trend here, success by association is no different than guilt by association. Don't just tag along with any family, as some families are not properly led, may be unhealthy or toxic, or may simply be a bad fit for you and your family. You have to pay attention to the dynamics, the fruit they produce, commonalities in morals and values, and whether they are in a place in their lives and career that you desire. It is a horrible idea to connect with or be mentored by a family on the brink of divorce, where one of the spouses constantly walks the line of infidelity, they have very little motivation to excel beyond their current careers in which they barely make ends meet, feel that just getting by is enough, and have no dreams or goals. It could result in deterioration of your marriage or relationship. I doubt that this is your desired status, therefore I encourage you to find someone who has a longstanding marriage that inspires you and is a good model and example to follow. Connect with people who will not hinder growth or distract you from your goals.

Whether it is business or family, having a "why" and remembering that "why" throughout the process is very helpful. Whether it is business or family, having a "why" and remembering that "why" throughout the process is very helpful. The factors that contributed to my "why" were my marriage, my children, wanting to make my parents proud, and my educational and career goals.

Meditating on your "why" will help you regain focus
when you lose it and maintain endurance
when you are fatigued.

I hope you are able to see a common trend or theme in this chapter. You achieve success by association. This is no different than the concept of guilt by association. I am not encouraging you to distance yourself from people you love that don't have the same goals as you. I am encouraging you to intentionally seek out people that can help you take every aspect of your life to the next level. Your desire to excel shouldn't be the only motivating factor in your friendships and associations. You should enjoy being around them, you should feel good when you are around them, and when you leave them, you should find yourself inspired, motivated, and ready to work towards your goals. Have you ever been around such inspiring people that make you want to go straight to the lab, office, or studio and get right to work? Have you ever been around someone who makes you feel like you can accomplish everything you have put on paper, to the extent that when you left them, you went straight to work, and worked nonstop for hours afterwards? These are the people you should spend more time with. Once you have achieved your goals, are running a successful business, and have a healthy family, you should strive to be that person for someone else.

> *To whom much is given much is expected.*

You can't achieve greatness by following people who are negative, can't get along with others, are self-centered, want to see you succeed as long as you don't soar above them, want others to like you as long as they don't like you more than them, want others to celebrate you as long as they don't celebrate you more than them, and want to contain or limit the extent of your success to them, or to their benefit and comfort level.

> *You have to connect with people that understand and live by the principles that your success is their success, and when you look good, they look good.*

They believe that there is enough room for everyone to win, partnerships and collaborations are necessary, and competing with the people in their inner circle simply isn't necessary because you are all on the same team. Connect with people who are already doing what you want to accomplish, but not if you can't refrain from being jealous and malicious. A jealous and arrogant mindset has ruined a lot of personal and business relationships and can be addressed in therapy. That type of thinking is quite dangerous as it can cause a great deal of mental, spiritual, and financial damage to everyone involved. Make healthy connections, face yourself and address your personal unresolved issues, have fun, work hard, and be motivated and inspired to be great!

XV.

Chapter XV.

Nutrition and Exercise

We need to be in good mental and physical shape to complete the tasks associated with maintaining a healthy and intact family, while pursuing our careers and businesses. Learning to put the right nutrients in our bodies is a major part of endurance training. Proper nutrition will ensure we have the energy and health needed to do the work we do everyday. In addition, it will help maintain a healthy body weight, while reducing the risk of fatigue and disease. We have all witnessed many successful people become ill in the midst of their most successful years and be required to take a break from their career to manage the illness. This can result in costly setbacks, and possible inability to complete the race, just like failure to prepare and train for the right race can.

> *Taking care of our bodies and minds*
> *by practicing good nutritional habits*
> *is an essential component*
> *of achieving our dreams and success.*

You simply can't be at the top of your game if you are not well. Did you know that the food we eat can improve or worsen our mental health status? Let's start with the dark leafy greens. We have always been told to eat our vegetables, and we have watched Popeye become superhuman as a result of eating spinach. I would like to paint a different cartoon for you. How about the average human being such as yourself, who faces a daily challenge to get out of bed, struggles through life fatigued and worn down, now suddenly has energy to tackle daily tasks, is energetic enough to be emotionally available for their family, has the energy to run, grow, and promote their business, and is able to enjoy life again.

Many researchers and professionals from the medical community suggest dark leafy vegetables attack cancerous and precancerous cells, fight against inflammation in the body, and contain vitamins A, C, E, K, minerals, and phytochemicals. Depression has been linked with inflammation of the brain, therefore eating foods that reduce inflammation is a good idea. Walnuts and various seeds are high in omega 3's, which support healthy brain function, hence reducing symptoms of depression. Foods such as mushrooms, beans, tomatoes, onions, and berries are also effective in managing symptoms of depression.

> *You can find more valuable information*
> *about healthy nutrition in my book, titled:*
> **NURTURE YOUR BODY**
> **OVERCOMING AND PREVENTING OBESITY**

It will help improve your physical and emotional well-being through nutrition and living a healthy lifestyle. I want you to have the energy, health, and endurance to achieve a life so exhilarating, that future generations in your family will remember your name and tell their children and grandchildren about the great things you did while living that exhilarating life.

FITNESS

Since this is not a fitness or nutrition book, I won't spend too much time on the topic, but I can't write a book about living your best life and fail to make sure you understand how daily exercise will help you achieve that.

Exercise is an essential part of success.

If you have studied other successful individuals you will find that a large percentage of them get up early in the morning and exercise before they start their day. Poor health, low energy, disease, high risk for disease and obesity, will hinder your progress in business, family, and life overall. If anyone tells you being overweight or physically unhealthy is not an impedance to achieving your life goals, they are being dishonest with you or they lack in understanding the stress and problems that come with obesity. No one suffering from obesity wants to remain obese and experience the related struggles. This is unfortunately a form of discrimination, but a reality of life.

Although times have changed a bit, look at Hollywood! The people who climb the ladder to success most rapidly are people who at least appear to have taken care of themselves, have a healthy body mass index, and look like they are capable of completing the task at hand. There are many successful individuals in Hollywood that are overweight, but they aren't the majority. There have been many celebrities in the film and music community with successful careers and a promising future that ended way too soon, due to failing to live a healthy lifestyle.

Over time, obesity causes damage to the heart and other organs and puts you at risk for premature death. Rapid weight gain is also strenuous on the heart, so it is important to consistently maintain a healthy weight. Obesity promotes a poor quality of life and reduces the chances of success in all core areas of life. This does not mean it is impossible to achieve success in life while battling poor health or obesity, it simply means being overweight reduces the chances and adds complications.

> *I strongly encourage you to get healthy so you can crush your goals and stick around long enough to enjoy the fruits of your labor.*

I find it negligent to tell you how obesity can result in poor quality of life without sharing the risks associated with being emaciated or dangerously underweight. To be honest, the lifestyle you live, your cardiovascular health, whether you exercise daily, get proper rest, hydration, and nutrition have much more of an impact on your overall health, than how much you weigh. I know some of you will gasp at this statement, but being thinner does not always mean healthier. There are many people out there that are thin because they have not taken care of themselves and have robbed themselves of proper nutrition, because they weren't familiar with the main principles of a healthy lifestyle.

Recent studies have shown that in many cases, thinner women are dying earlier than their heavier counterparts. I suspect much of this is due to poor nutrition, which can result in inability to fight disease. As I mentioned in my first book, *Nurture Your Body - Overcoming and Preventing Obesity,* there are many foods that we should be eating to help fight disease. Food is your biggest defense against illness, inflammation, and toxic buildup in the body. If you fail to give your body the nutrients and defense that it needs against disease, you are increasing your risk for poor health. Another possible explanation for thinner women dying prematurely is the likelihood that many of them are taking weight loss pills, and other substances that are harmful to major organs such as the heart, liver, and kidneys. Many diet pills and supplements on the market are not regulated, FDA approved, and are harmful to your health. Unfortunately, many people don't learn which supplements are unhealthy and damaging until they have tried them, and their physical health has suffered as a result.

> *Everything you wish you could do,*
> *would like to do, dream to do, or plan to do*
> *needs to be written down.*

As I conclude this book on living an exhilarating, productive, purposeful, and successful life, I encourage you to WRITE. You will find that the journal created to accompany this book is a helpful tool in writing down your goals, reflections, thoughts, feelings, and tasks associated with your journey to living a life of exhilaration.

I still have the original notebook paper on which I jotted down possible names, services to be offered, and a basic outline sloppy copy of what *Club Exhilaration* would be and what we would provide.

Your Exhilarating Life will be filled with good health, happiness, and prosperity. Create it, build it, protect it, and share it with others!

ABOUT THE AUTHOR

Carmel Brown is a Certified Personal Trainer, a Certified Fitness and Nutrition Specialist, and Co-Owner of Club Exhilaration Fitness Center where she and her husband help their clients and members transform their bodies and their lives.

Carmel specializes in one on one training and business coaching, small group training, individual and group counseling and coaching, and meal planning. In addition, Carmel is a public speaker as she speaks, trains, and coaches at various events while helping her audience begin and maintain a healthy lifestyle, transform their bodies, improve mental health and emotional well-being, and ultimately improve their quality of life.

Carmel is also a Licensed Counselor which qualifies her to help clients push through mental and physical barriers to achieve a healthy body, healthy mind, and a transformed life.

For health and fitness coaching or counseling
visit the author website at:
WWW. CARMELBROWNCOUNSELING.COM

www.ingramcontent.com/pod-product-compliance
Lightning Source LLC
Chambersburg PA
CBHW062042200326
41519CB00017B/5113